T0065039

# GODS OF THE MORNING

'I love this book. It quickens the heart with hope and wrests real beauty from keen observations of the natural world. If only we could all be as attentive to the life around us as John Lister-Kaye. No one writes more movingly, or with such transporting poetic skill, about encounters with wild creatures. Its pages course with sympathy, humility, and wisdom'
Helen Macdonald, author of *H is for Hawk*

'*Gods of the Morning* is an exquisitely observed account of a year in the life of a Scottish glen, backed by a deep understanding gleaned through decades of study by a working naturalist, and homing in on the struggle the local wildlife is facing in coping with weather patterns that have become more and more unpredictable'     Neil Ansell, author of *Deep Country*

'The spirit of nature holds many unknowns, mysteries and magic. John Lister-Kaye questions these unknowns with perfectly crafted words, delving so deep that you can almost feel nature's pulse'
Colin Elford, author of *A Year in the Woods*

'*Gods of the Morning* is an extraordinary, beautiful and honest book by a writer of profound personal and scientific knowledge. Few books urge me to read them again but this is one of them'     Virginia McKenna

'John Lister-Kaye is a rare species – a respected naturalist and a consummate wordsmith. Whether in person or on the printed page, there is no one I would rather choose to guide me through the glens in search of Scotland's wildlife'     Brian Jackman

'John Lister-Kaye is one of the most joyful, inspirational naturalists I know'     Kate Humble

'*Gods of the Morning* is a rich treasury of secrets stolen from the Highlands, seen through the eyes of a great naturalist'     Chris Packham

Also by John Lister-Kaye

# GODS
## OF THE
# MORNING

A BIRD'S-EYE VIEW OF A CHANGING WORLD

## JOHN LISTER-KAYE

PEGASUS BOOKS
NEW YORK  LONDON

GODS OF THE MORNING

Pegasus Books LLC
80 Broad Street, 5th Floor
New York, NY 10004

First Pegasus Books hardcover edition August 2015

ISBN: 978-1-60598-796-5

10 9 8 7 6 5 4 3 2 1

Printed in the United States of America
Distributed by W. W. Norton & Company, Inc.

For
Arthur Williamson
with love

'Let us haste to the cool fields, as the gods of the morning begin to rise, while the day is young, while the grass is hoar, and the dew on the tender blade most sweet to the cattle.'

*Georgics 3* 324 ff – Virgil

# Contents

# Preface

In all its incalculable ramifications and contradictions, nature is my love, and its study and interpretation – natural history – have been my life and my work for half a century. How many people, I often wonder, can indulge their private passion in their everyday job? I don't have to be told how lucky I am. But it doesn't end there. For more than forty years I have lived and worked surrounded by mountain scenery that can still stop me in my tracks, and by some of the most highly specialised wildlife to grace Britain's wild places. How many people in Britain today *ever* get to see a golden eagle?

In 1976 I set up a field studies centre here at Aigas, an ancient site in a glen in the northern central Highlands – it was Scotland's first. It is a place cradled by the hills above Strathglass, an eyrie looking out over the narrow floodplain of the Beauly River. Aigas is also my home. We are blessed with an exceptionally diverse landscape of rivers, marshes and wet meadows, hill grazings, forests and birch woods, high moors and lochs, all set against the often snow-capped four-thousand-foot Affric Mountains to the west. Golden eagles drift high overhead, the petulant shrieks of peregrines echo from the rock walls of the Aigas gorge, ospreys hover and crash into the loch, levering themselves out again with a trout squirming in their talons' fearsome grip. Red squirrels peek round the scaly, rufous trunks of Scots pines, and, given a sliver of a chance, pine martens would cause mayhem in the hen run. At night roe deer tiptoe through the gardens, and in autumn red deer stags surround us, belling their guttural challenges to the hills. Yes, we count our blessings to be able to live and work in such an elating and inspiring corner of Britain's crowded isle.

Yet, for me, the real joy and sometimes the pain of living in the same place for all these decades is that I have come to know it at a level of intimacy few can achieve, and as a result the Aigas place has infiltrated my soul. Of course, in that time I have witnessed disasters as well as triumphs. We have lived through insensitive developments and land-use practices that have been profoundly damaging to the essential wildness of the glen and its wildlife. But we have also witnessed the return of the osprey and the red kite, and the pine martens have recovered from being one of Britain's rarest mammals when I first moved here to being locally common and a regular feature of our lives.

Birds have been at the heart of my work and my life. So much more visible than most mammals, they are my gods of the morning, lifting our days with song and character. But they have also been important thermometers of environmental health and change – not always a happy story. Like so many other places, we have lost our moorland waders: curlew, lapwing, greenshank and redshank all nested on our moors and rough pasture thirty years ago – none now – and the quartering hen harriers and short-eared owls have vanished with them. Even the oystercatchers, whose exuberant pipings used to be the harbingers of spring, have gone from the river.

Whether these dramatic shifts in wildlife fortune have been brought about by climate change alone, or whether the various seismic shifts in agriculture and forestry policy we have lived through have changed the nature of the land, or whether some more insidious cause lies hidden is very hard to guess at, far less to know. It could be, of course, that, as is so often the case in ecology, the combined impact of several factors colliding at once has made survival so unpredictable for so many species.

I am wary of blaming climate change for everything. In my opinion it has become a touch too glib an explanation for too many aberrations in long-established wildlife patterns, such as the arrival and departure of migratory birds; a convenient get-out for those who are not prepared to admit that relentless human pressure on the globe and its natural resources has always brought about the extinction of species and the destruction of their habitats. That is what humankind has always done. But I cannot deny that in the last few years it would appear that the pace of climate change has accelerated and we have entered a period of total weather unpredictability.

We have no idea from one year to the next whether the summer will be hot and dry or dismally cold and wet; whether winters will be absurdly mild or gripped by snow and ice, or what extremes of heat or chill we can expect. We can no longer predict how successful our common breeding birds will be – the swallows didn't bother to nest

3

in 2012 – and we aren't the only ones kept guessing and bewildered. Some wildlife can adapt quickly; others fail and disappear, with us at one minute and gone the next.

This is a book of encounters, observations and speculations based on what I have witnessed around me in my time. It attempts to explore how some of those changes have affected our common and not-so-common birds, their breeding successes and failures, their migratory arrivals and departures, their interactions with us and their populations around us. In the way that they respond quickly to shifts in climate and human behaviour, birds are also important and visible monitors of the success and failure of other wildlife, especially invertebrates. We dismiss or ignore these signals at our peril.

This book also focuses on some of our special Highland wildlife, mammals as well as birds, as perceived every day through the shifting seasons of a year by a working naturalist, perpetually looking, listening, watching, probing and taking notes, or, as my wife, Lucy, would say, with a shake of the head and a sigh of long-sufferance, 'totally distracted'.

I have no answers. I am as bewildered by what appears to be happening as anyone else, although I am suspicious that man's addiction to fossil fuels and our obsessive rush for wealth at any cost during and since the Industrial Revolution may have accelerated and possibly caused the systemic instability in our global weather systems, which may yet prove to be our nemesis. Yet living and working closely with wildlife, and birds in particular, has enabled me to witness some direct effects and thereby share some experiences and pose some questions of my own.

4

# I

# Blackcap

Sitting calmly, embowered in thick foliage, he pours forth, without effort, a delightful flow of soft and pleasing melody; then suddenly elevating his voice, he warbles aloud a cheering, liquid strain, which, at least in these islands, is unrivalled.

> *The British Cyclopaedia of Arts, Sciences, History, Geography,*
> *Literature, Natural History and Biography,*
> Charles F. Partington (ed.), 1838

Autumn already! So why dismiss the everlasting sun, if we are sworn to search for divine brightness – far from those who die as seasons spin . . .

> 'Farewell', Arthur Rimbaud

Yesterday a small bird flew into my study window and died instantly. The soft thud, barely audible, lifted my head as I sat at my desk in the afternoon sunshine. It was loud enough for me to know that it was a bird and that it had meant almost certain death. I tried to return to my work, but couldn't. My spirit plunged.

These deaths occur far too often. We have tried hanging CDs in front of the windows, sticking hawk silhouettes to the panes, moving bird tables and feeders away from windows, but to little avail. Every year a toll of winged victims falls to window strike: tits, sparrows, chaffinches, siskins, greenfinches – even, occasionally, the heavier *dunt* of a blackbird or a thrush shatters my concentration and brings me, sighing, to my feet.

A few years ago a collared dove powered into the glass. Its neck snapped instantly, and the force of the strike flattened the whole bird against the pane, head, breast, wings outstretched, so that a pale ghost was left imprinted on the window in the oily bloom from its feathers. I left it there for weeks, hoping it might deter others.

They see the sky reflected in the glass and fly joyously at its illusion of freedom. They're heading out: that's why they're flying so fast, so purposefully and so fatally. Occasionally, after a spell of dazed concussion, a bird recovers and flies uncertainly away to a bush or a tree, but all too often I have held them in the palm of my hand and felt the tiny heart flutter to a halt; far too often, I've watched the eyes mist in a slow, final eclipse.

So, yesterday I rose from my desk and went outside. The tiny form lay directly below the window, like a small grey leaf. I bent to pick it up and found that it was a blackcap, a male blackcap, the little *Sylviid* warbler that graces our gardens every spring and summer with a cascade of song, haunting in its tender melancholy, as melodious as a flute and as rich as plum cake.

It shouldn't have mattered what it was. Is not a sparrow's life equal to that of a blackcap? ('Are not two sparrows sold for a farthing . . .?') A siskin equal to a blue tit, a greenfinch to a chaffinch? But it did. I have revered that song ever since blackcaps first arrived here in our northern Highland glen some twenty-five years ago. Back then they were exciting new arrivals, southern birds we didn't expect to see or hear in the Highlands at all. But something was permitting them to colonise new ground; some shift in climate or food supply gave them a new niche they were quick to grab. We came to know them as summer visitors slowly edging their way north, year on year, until finally they were no longer unusual.

They became a seasonal norm, belonging here, warbling ecstatically from every clump of brambles or willow thicket, a virtuoso exhortation to the songscape that awards passion to our spring and splashes musical glamour on the dull face of our summer. And they changed me. I came to long for their arrival every May and mourned their sudden absence every autumn. Without my realising it, blackcaps had warbled their way through my auditory meatus like a drug, imprinting on my subconscious so that I dreamed of them at night and awoke to their song in the dawn.

Sometimes if I stood still in the garden I would catch sight of one flitting nervously from branch to branch, hawking invisible insects high in a sycamore canopy or deep in a thicket. Through binoculars I could tell the sexes apart: the male with his little black *kippah* and the female's in rusty red. They became real companions, like trusted neighbours you would always cross the garden to chat to. And always that refrain brought a smile to my face; sun or rain they made me happy to be out there, sharing my life with such exuberant songsters.

7

To hold this one dead in my hand, limp and still hot, summarily silenced, its eyes shut and slender bill clenched, seemed to me yesterday to be a tragedy greater than normal – if one can detach sufficiently to accept the death of garden birds as normal. I felt empty, hollowed out by an overpowering sense of injustice.

Then I realised it was September. I'd thought they had gone. The song had stopped a few weeks back. For several mornings I had stood at my open bedroom window staring out at the dawn, waiting for the blessed refrain to burst. All I'd got was a robin, 'the first god of the morning'. I love robins too – and, for heaven's sake, they do their best. They stay with us all year and keep going, always first at dawn and last at night, come frost or snow, driving sleet or bright blue sky. I do not mean to slight them. But for me they are outclassed by this little warbler – a morning deity if ever there was one – that some consider a rival for the nightingale.

I looked closer at the tiny corpse in my hand. Was it adult, or a youngster? A late fledgling that never made it to migration? I opened a fawn wing, blew gently up the breast feathers to see if there was the slightest hint of down. No clue. I knew only that it appeared to be a fully grown male, its cap as dark and glossy as liquorice. Yet in its death it had taught me something new. Blackcaps stop singing some weeks before they depart. And, as is the coda for all natural-history study, its death posed more questions than answers.

Was it young or old? Had it done its work? Had it mated and raised a brood, multiplied itself, fired the blackcap future with its warbling genes? If so, would its offspring return to our patch, snatch aphids from our aspens, bugs from our brambles, sip sugars from our wild fruits? Questions I couldn't answer. I could only hope that this tiny, untimely death was not entirely in vain, that good would somehow come of it.

When we were children, with an irony wholly unimagined, we buried such corpses with ponderous funereal ceremony and erected little crosses to mark the passing of our pet mice or guinea pigs, birds like this one or fledgling orphans we had failed to raise. We were sublimely unaware that we were completing the cycle of all living things, of returning nutrients to the earth whence they came. I took the blackcap to a spiky and impenetrable *Pyracantha* thicket and tossed it gently in. Just the sort of place it might have chosen for itself.

★    ★    ★

That was yesterday. Today it dawned on me that the black-caps had been one of the few normalities of our year so far. They had arrived, played out their particular summer pageant and now, as the first mists wafted over the river and the loch, and the first frosts crisped my footprints on the lawn, they were about to depart again, to slip away in the dawn, to chase the dwindling bug swarm south to England, over the Channel to Belgium, on to Germany, whispering unseen through the high passes of the Alps and down into Spain and Italy, all far more productive climes for the bugs, seeds and nectar they need.

This autumn departure is one of the very few normalities of our seasonal Highland story, a standard by which to measure what has otherwise made 2013 an extraordinary year. That little warbler had fired something in my brain and caused me to write this down, and that departure, as the season wafted silently away from summer, was where I needed to start. Perhaps, after all, its death was not entirely in vain.

## 2

# That Time of Year

That time of year thou mayst in me behold
When yellow leaves, or none, or few, do hang
Upon those boughs which shake against the cold,
Bare ruin'd choirs, where late the sweet birds sang.

'Sonnet 73', William Shakespeare

You would think, wouldn't you, that the logical and proper place to start was January: the freshly washed face of a new year? But in all due deference to the double-faced Roman god Janus, the god of beginnings and transitions, I must point out that his month is of rigidly human designation and precious little to do with nature. It misses the plot. Whoever plumped for naming it was not thinking seasons or wildlife or weather, or even, with months of winter yet to endure, the human spirit. January may be the beginning of the Gregorian calendar year, but it is hardly a month of transitions.

It straddles the plunging nadir of the Highland winter; it records our most gripping frosts down to −25° Celsius when diesel fuel turns to jelly, your skin instantly sticks to metal and, of course, January snows, from a powder dusting to drifts of three feet, are always just around the mountain. Even in mild winters when a warm Atlantic airstream clashes with a front of Continental cold we are raked by sudden storms of swirling sleet, despite the most valiant efforts of the Gulf Stream, huffing and puffing like the big bad wolf on the western side of the mountains. Not much transition there.

January is when the chimney moans as south-westerly gales howl through the trees and hammer at our door. It is the month of brief, crimped days when the dogs won't stir from their baskets; the month of thick gloves, neck-hugging scarves and fur hats, of tightly drawn curtains and glowing firesides; it is the month of hunkering down and staying put. Many mornings I have arisen in the dark, peered out of the window into whiplash sleet or icy rain squalls so fired with spleen that I have chosen to crawl back to bed rather than face the world.

Neither, of course, is it the beginning of anything but the eponymous month. So, to do justice to nature, the nature of this mystical land of hills and glens, forests, lochs and rushing rivers, and to the confused seasons of what has proved to be a discomfiting and bizarre year, I need to start at a real transition, in late September when fidgets of swallows were gathering on telephone wires like chittering clothes-pegs; when the first tug of departure was fizzing in blackcaps' tiny brains; before moonlit frosts cantered rust through the bracken; before the chlorophyll finally bled from blushing leaves; even before the last osprey lifted and wheeled into its long migration to Senegal or the Gambia. I need to start when the word was fresh on our lips, in the incipient, not-quite-sure-if-it's-happened-yet autumn of 2012.

Autumn may arrive slowly, but it gives itself away.

Something ethereal arrives in the night, some curious edge to the breeze, some abstract quality of the breathed air, so that when you step outside you just know in your bones that the whole world around you has shifted its focus from summer and is now interested only in preparing for winter.

It is a climacteric, a moment of physiological and psychological shift in nature's thinking, especially for the birds. Summer birds depart, winter migrants begin to arrive. In the Highland glens, bird numbers plummet as their food supplies – natural fruits and every kind of creeping, crawling, slithering or flying bug – begin to disappear. Not just the swallows and house martins have vanished from round the houses. Gone are the insect-snatching wheatears, whinchats and stonechats from the hills; redstarts and flycatchers have fled the woods. Pied wagtails no longer flicker across the lawns, while sandpipers and grey wagtails have deserted the riverbanks. Farmland and hedgerow species have vanished in the night: the linnets, yellowhammers, and all the warblers have decamped from the thickets. By the first frosts the hills will have emptied to a few hardy stalwarts, such as the golden eagles, the raven and the irrepressible hooded crows. Silence settles across the land. The few species that are left frequent a changed world. Soon only the buzzards and wood pigeons will hang on in the woods, and the coniferous forests will host flocks of chaffinches, tits, siskins and crossbills passing through.

Waders from Russia, Scandinavia and the Arctic will flood to our shores and flotillas of ducks and geese will gather on the tidal mud – but I am getting ahead of myself.

On a full moon the temperature plunges overnight, a

careening splashdown to zero as the Earth's heat soars to the Milky Way. By dawn Lucy's dahlias have collapsed at the thought, the last nasturtiums have flopped like burst balloons and the stinging nettles are hanging their heads, like convicts awaiting execution – they know their number is up. Even if we are blessed with an Indian summer for a week or two in October, the natural world isn't fooled for long. There is urgent business afoot. To ignore the signals and loiter is to court disaster. Suddenly everything has changed.

\*　　\*　　\*

A dank drizzle settled over the Highlands. By dawn the river had risen from a whisper to an urgent murmur. Mists shrouded the dark flow and clung between the bankside alders well into the morning. We awoke to a damp, rusting-away world of yellow and umber. The shortening days seemed to be draining the paling chlorophyll with them. Trails of fieldfares and redwings chattered across the sky and descended like archangels onto rowan trees now bright and laden with scarlet fruit, hurrying, stripping them bare, moving on in undulating squadrons as though they had some pressing appointment elsewhere.

Later the sun came sidling in. It is low now, its power vanquished, enfeebled by the year's reeling. It will track a lower path every day until midwinter, 21/22 December, the winter solstice and the longest night, when, imperceptibly at first, it will begin to lift again. At our latitude, north of the 57th parallel, a laggard sun rises late in midwinter and barely lifts above our hilly horizon, sloping off as soon as it can, by about three in the afternoon. Cool and remote, it's a token appearance, a mere gesture to remind us that spring and summer will, with luck, one day return.

At eleven this morning it cut swathes of gilded light into the trees and across the green lawn, absorbing all the colours into one glorious October gleam charged with a cool and ruthless beauty. I stepped from shade into its glamour, then back again to see if I could detect any warmth. I could, but only just. That alone should be enough to tell the natural world to hurry along, to wrap up and get ready for what is to come.

Yet it is the intensity of the light that dictates the radiance of the autumn leaf colour. Leaves absorb red and blue wavelengths from sunlight, reflecting the green light to us. Green is good. Green tells us the tree is alive and well. If something goes wrong, such as a drought, the leaves begin to yellow because the green chlorophyll is no longer being fed, causing it to break down. It can't absorb the red light any longer, so it gets reflected outward to our eyes. It is this mixture of red and green light that creates the yellow. The loss of green is a biochemical phenomenon with high, show-stopping drama and profoundly poetic consequences.

Autumn colour is the universal manifestation of the same process. Dictated by plant hormones, as the length of daylight recedes, the water and minerals, especially phosphate, that have fuelled photosynthesis all summer long, are cut off in deciduous plants at the stem of the leaf. The powerful green pigment in chloroplasts, *chlorophyll* – which, as every biology pupil knows, is the essential component for converting sunlight into sugars and is responsible for what John Cowper Powys described as 'an enormous green tidal wave, composed of a substance more translucent than water, has flowed over the whole earth' and what I call the 'great green stain of summer' – begins to fade because it can no longer replace itself.

Without the supply of water and phosphate, chlorophyll burns itself up and disappears, allowing other pigments that are always there but drowned by the green wave, to begin to show through. These are principally *carotenoids*, bright yellows and oranges, and *anthocyanins*, the reds and purples, hence the drama and the rush for the poet's pen. But their celebrity is brief: they, too, are doomed to the same fate as the chlorophyll, which is why this whole process is uncharitably dubbed 'autumnal senescence'.

As the nights grow steadily cooler, the anthocyanins are responsible for removing sugars from the leaves the tree is about to shed. Only when the leaf is of no further use to the tree do the leafstalks grow cork cells to close off the conductive veins with plugs of special water-absorbent tissue. These freeze with the first frosts and the cells burst open, causing the leaves or needles to fall.

Bucking the trend, our oaks and beeches lose their chlorophyll like the rest, but stubbornly refuse to drop their leaves, an esoteric adaptation known to botanical boffins as 'marcescence'. No one knows quite why this is, but there are several plausible theories. Some say the dead leaves hide the new buds and deter damage by herbivores, such as deer, evidenced by the measurable observation that the lower, younger branches, those within browsing reach, hold their leaves longest.

Others proffer subtler and rather more imaginative hypotheses that retained dead leaves collect snow, which acts as an insulating blanket to protect developing shoots in the depths of winter and also hold it longer in the spring thaw, thereby providing a water supply to their roots at a time when the ground may dry out too rapidly for the tree's comfort. I find that idea challenging. Yet others have proposed that the dead leaves contain sugars that will better benefit the mother plant if released in the spring when the nutrients are most needed. The theory I consider the least likely is that oaks and beeches (hornbeams too) are slightly backward from an evolutionary perspective – less biologically intelligent (the very suggestion!) – and haven't yet fully worked out how to shed their leaves quickly. Whichever is the case, or maybe none, I draw comfort from the notion that nature reveals its motivations only slowly; mysteries within mysteries that keep us arrogant, would-be know-alls firmly in our place.

\*   \*   \*

There is so much going on in October that there should be a better, more uplifting name for the passage of autumn into winter. The Mellowing, or the Misting perhaps, or the more intimate *double-entendre*, the Rustling. That's what I hear when I close my eyes and stand underneath the rookery at the end of the month. For the moment the rooks had upped and gone, leaving only a vapid sky and an unavailing silence behind them. I wouldn't expect them back permanently until February, but if they happened to be passing in their unruly troops, they'd occasionally drop in for a few hours and clog the trees with their quarrelsome bustling, like school-kids claiming their spaces well before the bell goes. But in today's soft rain they were absent, and the oaks and sycamores solemnly dripped in an uncluttered, graveyard silence. When I stood completely still, a transcendental moment with only the pluming of my breath to reveal my presence, the silence bent to a lower urgency than a rowdy rook could comprehend. Beneath my feet, all around me, busy, industrious life was at work.

I have often noticed that life beneath the rookery is fuller, richer and more diverse than similar habitats nearby. Logically, when you consider the rainfall of nitrogen-rich droppings from on high during at least five months of each year for well over a hundred years, coupled with the annually layered carbohydrate of mouldering leaves from the sycamores and oaks, it is hardly surprising that the soil is rich. Here, beneath the trees, despite the shade, the naturalising daffodils I have planted are always finer, taller, grander and a richer gold than elsewhere.

Off to my left, with quick, jerking thrusts, a blackbird was cashing in, flicking rusty leaves, as if turning the pages of an ancient tome in a rushed search for wisdom. A restless robin fluttered from the wooden fence to the ground and back again, always pert, chinking its little metallic assertions, always checking out where my footsteps might have delivered up a worm, a bug or a centipede. And somewhere invisible, somewhere under the wind-blown waves of leaf litter, a shrew was blindly burrowing in its own private, nose-quivering, bristle-trembling quest.

Everything alive knows that winter is coming. Everything needs to hurry, to feed, to lay down fat, to burrow down, to bore deep into the sanctuary of timber or soil, to crawl under stones, into hollow logs or mud, to build nests, to take in bedding, to batten down. Need and haste: those are the two bywords for this moment in the year. They are the apothegm by which so much survival hangs. The bell for last orders has sounded loud and clear. Even the moon seems to know it, as it rounds to its chilly apogee, trailing mercurial pallor across the lawn and freezing the shaggy world with an icing that crackles like fire beneath my morning feet. By the time the stifling snows and vicious frosts arrive, for many it will be too late. Nature takes no prisoners; it renders no quarter to the unprepared.

The red squirrels were busy building a new drey. I was watching one yesterday, scurrying (its Latin name is *Sciurus*). It was pruning fresh larch and pine fronds and bearing them along in its teeth, fronds sometimes fully its own length, then weaving them together with the practised eye of a gypsy wife making baskets, pushing, bending, pulling, intent, labouring away with paws and teeth, totally oblivious to, or more likely just ignoring, my silent presence a few yards from the foot of the tree. Time-served though they may be, my field skills cannot boast the fooling of a squirrel on high. It knew I was there, all right, but I was no threat to that tail-flicking, nose-twitching, bright-eyed red, busy about its urgent affairs. Only one thing burdened its mind: winter.

Earlier in the day I had watched two of these enchanting native squirrels at the nut box I had put out for them. (We have no pox-carrying greys in the northern Highlands yet – they haven't crossed Loch Ness – and I pray that we may have the resolve to keep them out.) They were busy feeding, laying down fat, but also carrying off the hazelnuts in their teeth and burying them with rapid, jerky forepaws, scrubbing out the shallow cache pit, carefully dropping the nut and filling it in again, even scattering a few leaves over the top, all in a matter of a few seconds. Then back to the box for more. What makes me chuckle at this important caching of winter supplies is the ritual furtiveness of the process: the casting-around to see who else might be watching, with the shifty look of a shop-lifter about to pocket something, the nipping off to a quiet corner, the frantic digging, then more furtive glances while sitting upright on its tail for a better view, and scuttling back for another nut.

And the question I am so often asked: can they remember where they have buried the food? The evidence seems to be that they can – at least some of the caches. It would be a dangerous waste of energy and food if they couldn't. But undoubtedly some nuts survive to germinate and grow a hazel tree and the squirrels must be saluted for fulfilling that important, if accidental, ecological role. I am glad I saw them building that drey and I noticed that, whether by chance or design (surely design), it was built on the sheltered side of the trunk, away from the prevailing wind. Squirrels don't hibernate, so I find it a comforting thought that when the bitter winds slice through in the long December nights they will be in there, tucked up in their long fluffy tails, curled as tightly as a barrister's wig.

This moment in the year is also marked by the very sensible migration indoors of wood mice, *Apodemus sylvaticus*. Voles and shrews are fascinating, but wood mice are classy. Hamster-golden with huge ears and big glossy eyes as black as polished ebony, underbellies as white as the rose of York, and their extravagantly long tail (they used to be called long-tailed field mice) pursues them, never touching the ground, flowing with all the elegance and style of Elizabethan calligraphy. They skip across the ground with the grace of a gazelle, barely seeming to touch the surface, and they can climb and leap like a trapeze artist. I'm entranced by their speed. I have always admired them and, unlike Lucy when she's in hyper-efficient housekeeper mode, I am overcome by a downward somersault of the spirit when called upon to trap them. The notion of poison has always been abhorrent to me – out of the question.

There are times when I have had to set my natural-history instincts aside and give in to lobbying from household and family. After all is said and done, they are mice – beautiful mice – but with all the mouse potential for causing trouble. If they do become a nuisance and I am harried into taking action, I use Longworth live traps and transport the captives a few miles up the glen before releasing them, wishing them well and apologising as they go.

At first I made the mistake of thinking that releasing them in the garden was good enough until one day I caught one with the tip missing from his tail. The very next day he was back in the trap in my daughter Hermione's bedroom. I was pretty sure it was the same mouse so I took him much further away, about three hundred yards. Two days later he was back in the trap. To be certain I now marked his back with a touch of nail varnish between the shoulder blades where I reckoned he couldn't groom it away. I took him to the village a quarter of a mile to the east and furtively released him into someone else's garden. This time it took a week, but back he came, straight into the trap, proudly showing off his tell-tale smudge of oyster-shell pink. I was left scratching my head, pondering the mysteries of animal behaviour. Just how does a mouse, two inches high and six inches long, find its way over a quarter of a mile of what, presumably, must have been entirely strange and hostile territory? Is it scent? (We know that a male moth can detect a female's pheromones up to a mile away.) Or is it some electro-magnetic homing compass we don't properly understand? It seems entirely logical that any foraging species with static young in a nest must be able to find its way back over distances appropriate to that species. But a quarter of a mile? That seems absurdly adventurous for even the most ambitious mouse foray. And yet I know very well that I shouldn't allow myself to be surprised by this amateur circumstantial evidence of my own concocting.

Lucy once had a Labrador dog that was accidentally left behind at a friend's house some ten miles in a straight line from home. But those ten miles included crossing the Beauly Firth, a tidal estuary more than two miles wide, or a circumnavigation round the end of the Firth, increasing the journey to more than twenty miles. Frantic searches in the vicinity of the friend's house revealed nothing, but twelve hours later the old dog turned up at its own back door, wagging its tail. It was remarkable enough that he knew his way home, but that his homing instinct had caused him to swim across open sea or had taken him many miles in the wrong direction if he had gone round also seems to indicate some powerful impetus at work. I marvel at animal behaviour but it never surprises me. Nature has had a long time to hone its secret skills.

Throughout the spring and summer, these engaging little mice are more than happy to live in the woods and fields where they belong, and are one of several small mammal prey species upon which so much of our wildlife depends. Tawny and barn owls, foxes, badgers, wildcats, pine martens, stoats and weasels, buzzards and kestrels, even herons, crows and brown rats all eat wood mice when they can. With bank and field voles, they are the staple diet of our owls. Without them the owls would perish and disappear altogether. But the wood mice are hard-wired to find a warm, dry place to nest for the long cold months. We have generously provided them with an endless selection of choices: garden sheds, byres, stables, garages but, best of all, centrally heated houses, often with a fast food supply readily tipped in for good measure.

In this old house (some bits are eighteenth-century and earlier) the thick outer walls are of large round whinstones of hard metamorphic schist gathered from the fields and burn beds, heaved and levered into position by men with aching shoulders and rough hands, whose craftsmanship was passed down from generation to generation. However skilfully the Gaelic-speaking Highland masons placed these stones to create a handsome vertical wall on the outside, there were always hollows and gaps in the interstices that had to be packed with lime mortar to hold everything together. Inside the walls, which were always two or more large stones thick (up to twenty inches), there were spacious cavities loosely filled with end-of-working-day lime tossed in, along with any handy rubble. (While plumbing in new heating I once found a George I halfpenny dated 1718 in one of the walls – I'd treble your money for your story, Mr Highland Stone Mason, if only I could.) Lime mortar doesn't clench in a rigid chisel-resistant grip, like cement: it sets yet remains friable and crumbly, like damp Demerara sugar. Any diligent mouse can scrubble away at the weaknesses and burrow through.

Once inside the thick old walls, the mice enjoy a labyrinth all their own. They can go where they please. They travel through the hollows, up, down or sideways, as safe and secure as any city metro system. Modern insulation makes perfect bedding for a wood mouse – warmth and comfort laid on. At night I lie awake and hear them scuttling back and forth in the roof, up and down the ancient plaster and lath walls and occasionally popping up inside rooms. From time to time I see them nipping out from under the kitchen units to sample left-over meal in the Jack Russell terriers' bowls – a source of constant frustration to the dogs, which charge, skidding across the vinyl, to crash land among the bowls, always far too late.

We are lucky: our neck of the Highland woods does not have the very destructive and invasive house mouse, *Mus domesticus*, originally an alien species from Asia, trans-located all round the world by man, and the progenitor of all pet and laboratory mice, which can carry unpleasant diseases such as leptospirosis, typhus and meningitis – even bubonic plague. They are present in the Highlands, but mainly restricted to the grain-growing areas of the east coast and to towns and cities such as Inverness. Happily, they don't venture up the glens. House mice will gnaw through just about anything: lead and copper pipes, electrical cables, plastic, woodwork, plaster, skirting-boards and structural joists, even limestone.

Our wood mice, alas, are not entirely blameless: they delight in shredding polystyrene pipe insulation, and if they elect to nest in a wardrobe of stored clothes their actions can be very distressing. By comparison with house mice, though, the damage they do is slight. They are very clean living and are not known to transmit disease. When I find their nests in the woods, exquisitely crafted balls of grass, moss and leaves, often lined with sheep's wool, there is virtually no smell.

Years ago I brought some reindeer skins back from an expedition to Lapland. I thought they would make cosy bedside rugs for our growing family, but I was wrong. Reindeer fur has a fine woolly undercoat but the outer fur consists of longer, hollow, air-filled hairs for efficient insulation in an Arctic climate. These hairs are brittle. The regular passage of children's little feet broke the outer fur into a constant fall-out of shards, which stuck to everything, itched in their socks, clogged the vacuum-cleaner and drove their mother to drink. The pelts were banished to a cupboard in the cellar, securely contained (we thought) in sealed polythene bags.

The wood mice said, 'Thank you very much.' It took them no time at all to find the bags, nibble in and rearrange the rolled-up skins to their liking. Several months later, one of the field centre's education officers needed a piece of reindeer fur to demonstrate the efficiency of natural fur insulation to some visiting school-children. I opened one of the bags and was astonished to find that large patches of the pelt had been shaved clean down to the leather and the removed fur, both woolly and brittle, had been skilfully woven into an orb-shaped nest the size of a cantaloupe melon. On pulling it gently apart I found that the hairs had been systematically sorted and separated: the long hairs for the structure of the ball and the softer wool for the inner lining. The inside of the nest issued the essence of fertility, like leaf mould, making me think of wood anemones and unfurling ferns in spring – none of that uric rodent reek I remember from keeping pet mice as a boy. I was sorry I had disturbed it and put it back carefully, glad that they had found a use for the reindeer skins and happier to have them living in the cellar than in my wardrobe. It would be hard to imagine a warmer, cosier or more secure winter refuge from which to produce a family.

*     *     *

As I walked back to the house from the rookery, the unmistakable yelping chorus of geese floated to me on the damp air. I stood still and squinted into a sky of dulled metal. They were high, just below the ruffled cloud base at around three thousand feet; it took me a moment to locate them. There they were, in an uneven V-formation, shifting and flickering in a large wavering skein of tiny silhouettes, like flies on a high ceiling. I shivered. Not a shiver of cold – I was well wrapped – but a shiver of deep, transcendental unity. No sound in the world, not even the rough old music of the rooks, etches more deeply into my soul than the near-hysterical 'wink-winking' of pink-footed geese all crying together high overhead. It is a sound like none other. Sad, evocative, stirring and, for me, quintessentially wild, it arouses in me a yearning that seems to tug at the leash of our long separation from the natural world.

Their arrival in the early autumn sets a special seal on the turning year, repeated again with their departure, back to their Arctic breeding grounds in the spring when the last few rise, with rattling pinions, and wheel away into the north. Autumn or spring, I never tire of their unrestrained dissonance, which surrounds us during the winter months when tens of thousands of grey geese gather on the Beauly

Firth. Scarcely a day goes by without a skein or two passing over, or when we go east to the Black Isle, the moist coastal fields are always cluttered with their corn-gleaning and grass-plucking flocks.

It seems that naturalists (and perhaps not just naturalists) need these sounds to help us locate our passions, to ground us in the beliefs we hold about the natural world and to link us with our origins. My old friend Brian Jackman, the celebrated wildlife journalist, who has enjoyed a forty-year love affair with East Africa, tells me it is the night roaring of lions as he lies awake in his tent on the Masai Mara that does it for him. For Lennart Arvidsson, the half-Lapp-half-Finnish doyen of the Arctic forests, who first showed me wild lynx tracks in the Sarek snows, it is the long-drawn howls of timber wolves, rising and falling on a moonlit night. Dame Jane Goodall insists it is still, after nearly half a century since they catapulted her to world fame, the hoots and pants of a troop of chimpanzees deep in the forest that sets her blood tingling. Television wildlife cameraman John Aitchison recounts that, for all his globetrotting, it is the calls of waders – greenshank, curlew and redshank especially – on the Scottish salt marshes of his Argyllshire home in the crisp air of a morning in early spring that raises the hairs on his neck. And Roy Dennis, my ornithologist (and a brilliant all-round naturalist) colleague and friend of more than forty years, once told me that the combined fluting calls of tens of thousands of common cranes assembling on the wetland steppe of Hortobágy-Halastó in Hungary was a moment of pure transfiguration for him.

My geese and the shiver pass together. It is autumn, late autumn, and winter is no longer imperceptibly snapping at our heels. Its clawing fingers have finally gripped. I know there will be a piercing frost tonight. I pray that the rooks still gleaning manna from the barley fields are well prepared; bad luck for the hungry barn and tawny owls – I know that at least some of the wood mice have moved indoors. Like the robins and the blackbirds, the shrews have no choice: they have to keep going whatever the season, bound to the treadmill of twitching out from the dark confines of the leaf litter their own body weight of invertebrates every day.

The squirrels are well stocked up and these last, straggling goose arrivals will have joined the vast flocks that are gorging on the late spillings from combine harvesters on the stubbles of the Black Isle. A final few ash leaves gyrate silently to the yellow carpet of their own design. The crinkly oak leaves hang stubbornly on, only reluctantly releasing when winds scour through. And the silky-haired beech leaves will rattle like crisps until the spring when the new growth will finally force them off.

As I return to the house I see wood smoke pluming from a chimney. Lucy has lit the sitting-room fire, a sight that brings an inner glow and a smile to my tingling face. As the darkness closes in I shall repair to my old armchair with a book. The Jack Russells will yawn and sigh as they stretch themselves across the hearth rug at my feet. Winter brings blessings of its own.

# So Great a Cloud of Witnesses

Wherefore seeing we also are compassed about with so great
a cloud of witnesses . . . let us run with patience the race that
is set before us.

Hebrews 12:1

Those few last geese to arrive from the Arctic, straggling down
from the great heights at which they travel, often many thousands of feet, are special to me not just because I love to catch
their excited voices on the wind and see their silhouetted
chevrons against the clouds, but because they are living, crying
witnesses to nature's biorhythms present within us all.

We all migrate. We venture out and we return home. We
send forth our young. The winged seed spiralling to Earth
from a sycamore or an ash; the rowan berries ingested by
Scandinavian fieldfares and redwings are cast to the hills; the
lonely 'outcast' badger that dug himself a temporary home
among the roots of one of our western red cedars last year;
the spiders I witnessed ballooning down the wind on their
silk threads; the rooks and jackdaws I was watching this
afternoon, surfing the wind over the river fields; the swallows and house martins swooping low into the stables each
spring; the salmon surging up the Beauly River to spawn
every summer – all of these and myriad more organisms

around my home, around all of us all the time – are responding to the secret codes emitted by the sun and the spinning Earth, received and processed to serve each species' individual ends. 'So great a cloud of witnesses.'

They're heading out, patiently running the race their needs have set before them. They all need to feed, to breed and to survive, like surfers riding the waves of Fate. I, sitting tapping these words into my laptop, and you, reading them – whoever we are, wherever we may be and whatever our private pretensions – are also part of that same grand opera: the pull of life's imperatives. We migrate, whether a few yards before finding a suitable place to put down roots or circumnavigating the globe, like the Arctic tern, which travels ten thousand miles to the Antarctic and back again every year, patiently making the most of our lot, our personal shout at the survival of ourselves and our species. That's what migration is.

These days we understand it – at least, quite a lot of it. Seasonal bird migration in particular has been well and widely studied. We now know, for instance, that migration can be triggered by temperature, by length of daylight hours, by weather conditions and by diminishing food supplies, but we also know that it is genetically controlled. Glands churn and swell, hormones swirl. The imperative to get up and go when we need to is written into the electrochemical circuitry of human brains as well as bird brains.

In the case of geese, intricate studies have demonstrated that their innate circuitry and navigational skills are added to year on year by experience. Old birds get canny: they learn to read the wind. They know exactly the right moment to head off, and the youngsters follow. I've always loved the expression 'wise old bird'. It's never truer than of mature geese, sometimes individual birds that have made their twice-annual trek more than fifty times. A ringed (banded) snow goose hatched in Alaska and wintering in Mexico has been recorded still migrating at twenty-six years old – that's more than 130,000 miles of reading the wind. I ask myself just what huge range of conditions and changes, trials and close-calls lurk behind the twinkle in that wise old bird's eyes.

We also know that different families of birds respond to and navigate by different signals, reflecting each species' needs and capabilities and determining their route and desti-nation. Experiments in planetaria have proved that some *Silviid* warblers, such as the blackcap, are genetically wired to navigate by the stars, requiring them to migrate at night. Artificially exposed to different seasonal constellations, caged birds become restless and flutter to the north or south, according to their migratory instincts. Other species can detect the Earth's magnetic field or memorise significant landmarks, such as coastlines, river valleys and mountain ranges. Yet others follow the sun, demonstrated by German ornithologist Gustav Kramer's 1950s experiments with caged starlings. Most significantly, he proved, with mirrors and artificial cloud effects, that it wasn't direct sun they required, but that sufficient light intensity was all they needed for the correct orientation – an important ability for birds since the sun is so often obscured by clouds.

One of the most remarkable experiments in bird

navigation was conducted by my late great friend Ronald Lockley, a real pioneer of ornithological research and author of the ground-breaking monograph *Shearwater* (1946) – a study of Manx shearwaters nesting on the island of Skokholm off the Pembrokeshire coast of Wales. He took mature birds from their nesting burrows, then shipped them off to Venice and to landlocked Basel in Switzerland, many miles from any normal shearwater habitat or migratory route. They were back in their burrows fourteen days later.

Another bird was flown across the Atlantic to Boston, Massachusetts, some three thousand miles from home; a starting point completely unknown to that shearwater species. It took just twelve days to arrive back on Skokholm. What Lockley's experiments proved conclusively was that shearwaters must use navigational aids other than landmarks. What we now know is that birds often employ a combination of abilities: stellar, solar, geo-magnetic and geographical recognition, to locate themselves and return to precisely the same wood, moor, field, tree or bush, swamp, stream, burrow or cranny they departed from many months before. Our swallows swoop home from Africa to the rafters of their birth through the same door in the same stable at approximately the same moment, year after year. Nowadays we know so much that we take bird migration for granted, but it was not always so.

In the early sixteenth century the Bishop of Uppsala, Olaus Magnus, was convinced that swallows and other similar birds spent the winter months under water or in deep mud. In his *Historia de Gentibus Septentrionalibus* he goes so far as to cite the evidence of fishermen landing a catch of swallows in their nets. He was sufficiently persuaded by this bizarre explanation for the sudden disappearance of swifts and swallows in the winter that he commissioned a woodcut illustration of the fishermen with their catch, thereby endorsing an entirely bogus scientific claim that would remain substantially unchallenged for the best part of a hundred and fifty years.

There were doubters and fence-sitters, of course, casting around for objectivity, such as Robert Burton, who wrote in his 1621 *Anatomy of Melancholy*:

> Do they sleep in winter . . . or lye hid in the bottom of lakes and rivers, *spiritum continentes*? so often found by fishermen in Poland and Scandia, two together, mouth to mouth, wing to wing, and when the spring comes they revive again . . . Or do they follow the Sun . . . or lye they in caves, rocks and hollow trees, as most think . . .?

Yet this thesis sat uncomfortably with the drip-drip of evidence coming in from ships returning to British ports from the Mediterranean and Africa with tales of exhausted swallows landing on rigging or on decks.

John Rae, the great English naturalist of the seventeenth century, editing *Willughby's Ornithologica* in 1678, certainly expressed doubt: 'To us it seems more probable that they fly away into hot countries, viz., Egypt or Aethiopia.' But others would have none of it. Even the great Swedish taxonomist Carl Linné (Linnaeus) was insisting as late as 1768 that Bishop Olaus's confident assertions, with all the authority of the Church, were correct – that they hibernated under water.

By the end of the eighteenth century the ever more divided world of science had split clearly into migrationists and hibernationists. Gilbert White, curate of Selborne, was well aware of the debate. His lengthy correspondence with the Hon. Daines Barrington (hibernationist) and Judge Thomas Pennant (migrationist), both eminent naturalists of their day and Fellows of the Royal Society (and from which correspondence much of the text of his 1789 *Natural History and Antiquities of Selborne* was gleaned), reveals strong influences in both directions, but White was canny and stuck to a much more cautious scientific approach: 'As to swallows being found in a torpid state in the winter in the Isle of Wight or any part of this country, I never heard any such account worth attending to.' But with the scientific objectivity that would make his natural history so famous (never out of print in 225 years), he also hedged his bets.

> I myself on the 29th October last (1767) . . . saw four or five swallows hovering around and settling on the roof of the (Oxford) county-hospital. Now is it likely that these poor little birds . . . should, at that late season of the year . . . attempt a journey to Goree or Senegal, almost as far as the Equator? I entirely acquiesce with your opinion – that though most of the swallow kind may migrate, yet that some do stay behind and hide with us during the winter.

Gilbert White's brother was chaplain to the British garrison on Gibraltar. Also a keen naturalist and a reliable observer, John sent his brother reports of swallows crossing the strait to Africa. This first-hand evidence enabled Gilbert to write back to the devout hibernationist Daines Barrington:

> You are, I know, no friend to migration; and the well-attended accounts from the various parts of the country seem to justify you in your opinions, that at least many of the swallow kind do not leave us in winter, but lay themselves up like insects and bats in a torpid state . . . But then we must not, I think, deny migration in general; because migration does subsist in some places, as my brother in Andalusia has informed me. Of the motions of these birds he has ocular demonstration, for many weeks together, both spring and fall: during which periods myriads of the swallow kind traverse the Straits from north to south and from south to north according to the season.

This may well have irritated Barrington, because shortly afterwards he published a damning paper utterly refuting the whole idea of bird migration. Although White was totally convinced that bird migrations were real, he was evidently puzzled by the late movements of some species, often well into November, but his admirable scientific objectivity would never permit him to reject altogether, without positive proof, the hibernation possibility. Right at the end of his life he was still instructing labourers to search for hibernating birds in winter. In April 1793, only three months before his death, he asked a neighbour to assist him in examining the thatch on an empty cottage in Selborne.

\*    \*    \*

Things are very different, these days. We possess an astonishing log of scientific knowledge about migrations of all sorts. Thanks to ringing (banding) and radio tagging, birds are perhaps the most studied, but so are elephants and polar bears, herds of antelope, the great wildebeest migration from the Serengeti across the Mara River, and the carnivores and scavengers that follow them; deer, like the caribou migration of the Alaskan tundra and their attendant wolf packs; whales and seals of many different species migrating to breed or feed; eels and basking sharks and many other migratory fish; reptiles, such as turtles and crocodiles; and, of course, insects in uncountable numbers. Billions of monarch butterflies migrate up to 2800 miles down the North American continent from Alaska to Mexico because they can't withstand the cold winters.

Some of the research aided by modern technology has revealed previously undreamed-of feats of endurance and ability. Imagine their surprise when the pilots of an Air India passenger jet found themselves flying alongside a large skein of bar-headed geese at thirty-two thousand feet, an altitude required every year as the geese cross the highest Himalayan peaks.

Radio transmitters have revolutionised bird research. Very recently, an electronic tracking device weighing less than a paperclip uncovered what is now thought to be one of the world's greatest bird migrations. It revealed that a red-necked phalarope, a tiny wader the size of a wagtail, migrated thousands of miles west across the Atlantic to the Pacific Ocean, a journey never recorded for any other European breeding bird.

Dave Okill, of the Shetland Ringing Group, fitted

individual geo-locators to ten phalaropes nesting on the Shetland island of Fetlar. When a bird returned to Fetlar in the spring, Dave was astonished to discover that it had made an epic 16,000-mile round trip during its annual migration – across the Atlantic, south down the eastern seaboard of the US, across the Caribbean and Mexico, ending up off the coast of Peru, taking the same route back. Prior to this, many experts had assumed that Scottish breeding phalaropes joined the Scandinavian population at their wintering grounds, thought to be in the Arabian Sea.

My conservation colleague Roy Dennis has hugely increased our knowledge of osprey, marsh harrier and golden eagle movements by attaching transmitters to young birds leaving the nest. The British Trust for Ornithology has done the same by attaching solar-powered radio tags to English cuckoos in an attempt to discover the route and precisely where our diminishing British cuckoo population spends the winter. The results have been illuminating and, for us, deeply disappointing. Aigas Field Centre sponsored one bird named Kasper; he made it to the Congo Basin for the winter, but perished on the way back in the spring – just our luck. Of the first five birds tagged in 2011, only two made it back to Britain.

Sophisticated modern radar can also accurately track the movement of small passerine migrants. We now know that most small birds migrate at below five thousand feet, the most popular altitude being two to three thousand feet, whereas flocks of waders choose to travel much higher, at twenty thousand feet. We can also measure speed of flight very accurately. Warblers, finches and other small birds commonly cover thirty to fifty miles a night with daytime stopovers to rest and feed, whereas swifts, swallows and house and sand martins regularly cover up to two hundred miles a day, preferring to roost at night and fly by day so that they can feed on flying insects as they go.

Raptors, such as ospreys and harriers, tend to move much more slowly, travelling by day and using thermals to spiral upwards so that they can glide for long distances before rising and repeating the process all over again. The exception to this rule may be falcons. Only twenty-four hours after it was ringed in Paris, a young peregrine falcon was gunned down on Malta, some thirteen hundred miles south, an average of fifty-four m.p.h. without stopping.

★     ★     ★

For me, here and now, migration means geese and swans, waders thronging the mudflats of the Firth and woodcock slinking into the woods. Our small summer migrants all vanished south long ago, but the onset of winter brings the Arctic species down to our more favourable climes. I lie awake at night, listening out for the haunting music of whooper swans bugling through the moonlight. Then, with the first frosts and an east wind, woodcock suddenly arrive in droves from Scandinavia and Russia, escaping the snow and ice.

It is a gamble. If, as seems likely, birds are triggered into migrating by the length of daylight, they must also assess the weather, choosing suitable conditions and the right wind to travel. Two years ago the Scandinavian woodcock got their timing horribly wrong. They arrived in the Highlands, which were gripped by an unseasonably severe November frost. There had been a light snowfall immediately followed by –18°C, even on the coast.

The land fell silent. The Beauly River froze over. The loch became gleaming glass in the low-angled sun, and huddles of disconsolate mallard sat about preening on the edge of the rigid marsh. There was nothing else to do. The ground and its snow crust, even in the sheltered woods, was as rigid as concrete. Woodcock are woodland waders with long probing bills for winkling invertebrates out of the litter layers of damp forest soils. Unable to break through, they starved. My good friend and colleague Peter Tilbrook, former Nature Conservancy Council and Scottish Natural Heritage director, who lives on the east coast at Cromarty, doesn't miss much. He phoned to tell me that migrant woodcock, which had just arrived, were starving in his wooded garden. They were so weak that he could pick them up.

In the Aigas garden there is a small patch of wet woodland where a spring rises. I have never known it dry and I have never seen it freeze solid, although in very hard winters the open pool has grown a skin of thin ice. The spring water seeps away into the soil beneath the spreading branches of 120-year-old, close-planted western red cedars, whose closed evergreen canopy provides a resin-scented arbour like a secret den – a place where my children loved to hide when they were small. Following a hunch after Peter's phone call, I went to have a look.

There they were. Three woodcock stood together on the

damp soil, their large black eyes in sculpted soot- and cinnamon-barred heads stared blankly at me. I backed off, reluctant to stress them any more than the weather already had. The ground was dotted with the pockmarks of their hungry probings. I prayed they were finding something to sustain them. They stayed there a week, until the anticyclone drifted back towards Norway and a mild west wind flooded in to free us up.

How did they find that lonely wet patch, I wondered, the only one in a world of ice? What tricky avian sensibility had led them to that secret place? Could they scent the damp soil over the heady essence of cedar resin? Had they been there before in hard times? Did one wise old bird tell the others? So many questions, so many riddles. Such a cloud of witnesses.

# 4

# And Then There Were Rooks

Above the dark and drooping world
Let the empty skies disclose
Your dear, delightful crows.

'Crows', Arthur Rimbaud

Crow realized God loved him –
Otherwise, he would have dropped dead.
So that was proved.
Crow reclined, marvelling, on his heart-beat.

'Crow's Theology', Ted Hughes

I can't claim any prescience; neither am I given much to
old wives' tales or pithy country aphorisms. An abundant
fungal flora or a heavy crop of rowan berries doesn't seem
to me to mean anything more than a bumper year for
fruiting fungi and rowan trees. When the greylags and
pink-footed geese arrive earlier than expected, harrowing
the September skies with their treble-pitched clamour, all
that it tells me is that the season in their Arctic breeding
grounds – Greenland, Iceland, Lapland – is turning, and
that their migratory instincts have fired a little earlier than
in some other years.

Not so Old Malkie, famous round here for his doom-laden predictions, when I bumped into him at the Beauly petrol station. 'That'll be the snow on the way any day now,' he gloomed, waving his walking stick to the puckering late-October clouds and shaking his platinum curls. (To my intense chagrin, three days later there was a sugaring of snow on the three-thousand-foot pyramidal crest of Beinn a' Bha'ach Ard [hill of the high byre], which impales our cloud-laden horizon to the west.)

Yet despite all the head-shaking and dark muttering by the nay-sayers and would-be country sages in our glen, it did not seem to me to follow that blizzards are imminent, that we are in for a harsher winter than usual or that the end of the world is nigh. But I *am* moved by the wholly unexpected.

In early November our rooks arrived back at their long-established nests in the tall limes, oaks and sycamores that line the Aigas drive. You couldn't miss them. They were their usual boisterous personalities, like inner-city youths: racketing, arguing, bossing, coming and going, flapping, cawing loudly and generally carrying on like – well, like rooks always will. They were nesting – at least, they were going through the unmistakable motions of nesting. They were paired off, gathering and stealing each other's sticks, repairing old nests and even building from scratch. But it was only just November. Now that *was* unusual. We don't expect the rooks to attend their nests until February, sometimes late February, if the weather is hard. But November?

It didn't last. In ten days they were gone again, flocking

away in rowdy gangs tangled with jackdaws, down to the potato and stubble fields recently harvested, the arable soils of the Beauly Firth as dark and rich as molasses, where they joined up with hundreds, perhaps thousands, of others from far and wide. I never did discover why they had arrived back at their rookery so unexpectedly, so absurdly early. It was as though they were feeling some collective corvid memory lapse and a need to check it all out, just to make sure they were still welcome there, like old boys and girls heading back to school for nostalgia's sake. I logged it away as odd and, as the New Testament has it, 'pondered these things in my heart'.

With hindsight I now know that something other was indeed up, although it took a long time to become clear to me. At a human level we tend to view and assess climate change by large events, not small ones. Hurricanes, cyclones, storms and cloudbursts, rampaging floods and withering droughts are the dramatic yardsticks by which we measure swerves away from expected 'normal' patterns of weather. It's hardly surprising: they come rampaging in and imperil us with their power and potential for disaster – or far worse. But in reality they are probably just the crescendos in the overture, the pushy high points of much more subtle shifts and pulses that are happening, *pianissimo*, all the time, most of which go unnoticed or at best recorded only by meteorological boffins with their noses pressed to electro-barographs and computer models.

In just a few weeks we would know that whatever unde-tected signal had triggered the rooks' unseasonal return to their nests was indeed part of some much grander orchestration, something much more all-encompassing, much more . . . yes, perhaps 'sinister' is the right word, after all.

★    ★    ★

Not just God, but I also love rooks: *Corvus frugilegus*, the very fittingly named 'foraging crow'. The onomatopoeic crow – *hrōc* in Old English, *rork* in Old Dutch, *craa* in Old Scots, all, including the word 'crow' itself, inflections of the distinctive *kraa* calls everyone immediately recognises. I love them for their dissonant, rough-edged, pub-brawl rowdiness, all of which, as one of my earliest childhood memories, is permanently etched into my cerebral cortex.

I need to come out and declare this now because so many people seem not to like rooks, lumping them together with every other crow and often refusing to acknowledge the many differences – although getting it off my chest feels a bit like owning up to some contemptible vice. Farmers grind their teeth and spit venom when packs of rooks swoop down, like brigands, to raid their winter barley fields, ripping the germinating seeds and the stash of protein-rich sprouts from the rain-sodden tilth, just like the old Scottish Border reivers, '. . . where all men take their prey'.

In a fit of rage a farmer near here felled a handsome spinney of mature Scots pines just to prevent the rooks nesting there, and another, also given to uncontrollable outbursts of anger against many aspects of the natural world, attempted to sue his peace-and-wildlife-loving neighbours for having the temerity to harbour a rookery in their trees. Even those who don't suffer loss of any kind further darken the rooks' iridescent blackness by ignorantly dismissing them as just 'crows', uttered with a sneer and all the disdain one might award to football hooligans or drug dealers; an ornithological unfairness equivalent to lumping swans together with geese or writing off fieldfares and redwings as just thrushes. In fact, of course, the crow family is famously diverse, even the black or nearly black ones on the British list: rooks, jackdaws, choughs, carrion crows and ravens differ widely in character, habits, appearance, diet and their manifold interactions with people. It is hard to argue that crows bring many obvious or tangible benefits to mankind, but then neither do most other bird species unless we gain pleasure from their songs, their colourful displays or from killing and eating them, little or none of which relate to crows. Rightly or wrongly, the crow family have long been cast in the villain role and little I can say will alter that.

But, for me, rooks are different. I love everything about rooks and I have clung to the emotive authority of their cries since infancy, when I knew no birds by name and saw them only as flickering glimpses in the great whispering beech trees through the bedroom window of my childhood home. So I am proud to have a rookery at Aigas. I get personal and possessive about them when they return from their winter forays to nest in my trees and surround our lives with their remarkably human and often comical racketing.

The Aigas rookery is very old. We know from the first-hand testament of an old lady (Helen Foucar, now long deceased), who spent her childhood holidays here more than a hundred years ago with guardian godparents, who in their turn had been here since the 1860s, that every May back then the young birds were shot at the point of fledging, as they perched on the edge of their nests, by local Highlanders, the estate workers whose perquisite it was to harvest and consume this seasonal bounty. But our rookery is probably much older than she or her guardians knew. (Although the rhyme is thought to allude to Henry VIII's sacking of England's monasteries during the Reformation, the 'Four-and-twenty blackbirds baked in a pie' might well have been rooks: they were commonly eaten by country folk right into the second half of the twentieth century.)

This centuries-inhabited house sits in a wider landscape largely denuded of its trees in the seventeenth and eighteenth centuries by a population of Highland people perpetually teetering on the precipice of a failed harvest and famine. All trees had a price not so much on their lofty crowns as on their hearty bowls and stalwart limbs, for structural timber, furniture or firewood, for charcoal or just ready cash, anything to stave off the crushing poverty of what we would now consider to be a third-world existence barely compatible with civilisation. Only when the majority of Highlanders upped and left for southern cities and the New World in the nineteenth century (more than eight thousand left from this narrow glen, Strathglass, a diaspora extending well into the twentieth century) did the trees return either by planting or by nature's unsleeping opportunism. Ours are the legacy of that era: mature oaks, limes, sycamores and one or two big ashes, along with the naturally regenerated native birches, Scots pines, goat willows, hazels, rowans and geans (wild cherries).

Every spring I look forward to the rooks' return to the rookery, to the soap opera of their constant bickering, sabotaging and thieving from their neighbours' nests. One large and now well-established nest high in the swaying tops of a mature lime tree is in full view from our bathroom window. I can lie in the bath and watch the daily machinations of their competitive, gangland twig war, drink in the rough old music of their calling, ponder the urgent electricity of instinct blending with guile drawn from the hard-edged experience of survival, the ultimate judgement of all living things. But it is from their flight that I draw the greatest delight.

When a wild wind comes calling, hustling in from the south-west like an uninvited guest, its warm, wet embrace rises and falls, wuthering down the mountains and whirling through the crowns of our tallest trees, building zest and power, so often the precursor to short, stinging rain squalls. My eyes immediately avert to the clouds, to the roiling snowy-grey constants that are such dependable tokens of our time and our place in nature. Their ever-changing back-cloth seems to complement the drama of the rooks' flight, bringing vibrant focus to their ragged black shapes and awarding purpose to their swirling patterns. More vividly than any television forecast or smart-phone app, the clouds and the rooks speak to me about the day ahead.

They seem to sense the west wind's arrival. Effortlessly

they lift off into the quickening breeze, crying out for the others to follow, circling, rising clear of the trees in a ragged pack, out over the river and the broad valley for the sheer glory, for the wild giving of it, as though it has been sent specially for them.

From my study window I watch black rags, like small yachts, tossing on a tumultuous sea. They lift vertically, towering in a whirling tangle of wings, only to fall again in a joyous tumble of free-fall, gyrating, rolling and sweeping up to do it all over again. No one can convince me it isn't fun – more than fun: it's a delight longed for after days of dreary doldrums. They are school-kids let out into the play-ground after a tedious lesson; racehorses led prancing to the field gate and released into spring pasture after days in a stable, heels to the sky. They fly with all the carefree abandon of a sheet of newspaper picked up and hurled willy-nilly along an empty beach on a stormy day.

The consequence of loving rooks is that I have come to care for their well-being. (Jackdaws and ravens too but, I have to confess, not so heartily the malevolent villains of the black pack, carrion or hoodie crows – 'Crow, feeling his brain slip,/Finds his every feather the fossil of a murder', Ted Hughes). When the crofters' arable crops in the little river fields of this strath began to decline in the 1970s – no more oats, turnips and potatoes lovingly planted, tended and harvested by bent backs and weathered hands, stoically buttressed by universal little grey Ferguson tractors – I worried that the rooks would suffer and leave. But they clung on. The sheep and cattle fields still delivered up a harvest of grubs and worms, bugs and beetles sufficient to stave off the rooks' departure.

I did notice that they spent more time away in winter, away on the wide arable fields of the Black Isle, stocking up on corn and barley shoots, gleaning energy enough to be back in February for nesting and raising a brood. The world around them constantly changes at the hand of man, sometimes beneficent, sometimes profoundly taxing, but rooks are resilient and supremely intelligent birds: quickly they learn to adapt to man's latest agricultural whim and, as a happy consequence, the Aigas rooks are with us yet.

Then there is the wonderful cacophony of rooks. Their vocabulary is so expressive and varied. It certainly isn't restricted to the rasping 'caw' so often dumped on them, although, of course, in a flock they can be world champions of the cawing cause when they need to be.

From my bath on a spring day, with the window flung wide, I can phoneticise at least fifteen calls. (I often wonder how many naturalists habitually keep binoculars in the bathroom and can indulge their interest from the comfort of the bath – not, as Lucy was quick to point out, the most arresting image.)

The commonest is the benchmark 'caw', but which I prefer to present as 'kaarr' or 'aarrr' with a flourish of canine growl at the end that is absent from 'caw'. A bird with an urgent message to impart repeats this over and over again, with a forward thrust of the head and open bill, wings akimbo, the whole body jetting the sound forward with a counter-balancing upward flick of the fanned tail to send it on its way.

Then comes a collection of similar but quite distinctive calls of similar tonal quality, but with differing consonantal emphasis: a short, sharp 'kork' or 'dark' and a stretched 'daaark', a muted 'graap', an even quieter 'grup' and still softer 'brup', uttered as an afterthought or an aside to some louder exclamation. But these would all appear to be communication calls tossed into the broader clamour of the rook din – the rook cocktail party – as opposed to more intimate exchanges taking place between nesting partners, to chicks or near neighbours.

These more conversational utterances call for a gentler tonal approach altogether, and a much wider choice of pitch. 'Rirrp', 'trip', 'braa', a high-pitched 'creek' and the disyllabic 'err-chup' and an 'err-eek' exclamation can emerge from the same rook within the same conversation. Then there is a sharp, wholly un-rook-like click or clunk, such as you might make with your tongue on the roof of your mouth, often repeated over and over again. All this is often accompanied by a low, drawn-out 'er-r-r-r-r-r-r-k', a sound better suited to a tropical jungle than a Highland glen, uttered from somewhere gullet-glottal, somewhere in the depths of the corvid syrinx, very easy to imitate by drawing your breath slowly into your chest across your vocal cords, an irritating sound I delighted in making as a small child in the full knowledge that it would annoy adults. Rooks can keep this up for several seconds at a time, often eliciting astonishment from friends and visitors: 'What on earth is making that noise?'

To me, to someone who loves rooks, these sounds are interesting and reassuring, but the overall generality of rook music (yes, I find them musical), when the rookery is in full nesting swing, when the fifty or sixty birds are constantly on the move, bickering and haggling, like Arab traders in a bazaar, crying as loudly as they can, thrilling the air with a living resonance, is as evocative and emotive a natural presence as the slow thunder of breakers on a shingle shore or the muffled silence of Christmas snow.

Just now our rookery has twenty-nine nests. Years ago, when gentle crofting agriculture in the glen delivered its beneficial nutrients to all manner of wildlife (we had lapwings, curlews, corncrakes, grey partridges and corn buntings here, all now long gone), the Aigas rookery rose as high as thirty-eight, but the gradual arable abandonment has taken its toll and twenty-nine now seems to be the most they can manage.

They are big nests, each one the size of a pumpkin jammed into a high fork. They are often very close, occasionally touching each other, the spread apparently governed by the availability of suitable forks rather than any other territorial imperative. They occupy five big sycamores in one cluster and two fine old English oaks, and then an outlying nest in the lime tree I view from my bath, a hundred and sixty yards as the rook flies, off to the west. This last is recent, only a few years old, whereas the others are decades established, repaired and rebuilt year after year in the same places.

At first I thought the new nest (claimed as 'my pair') was a welcome expansion, but extending my daily bath time (to Lucy's irritation – 'What *are* you doing in there?') just to spy, I became concerned. There are plenty of big trees to expand into alongside the main rookery, so why, I wondered, was this pair building so far away? Slowly I came to realise that something else was going on. The two birds responsible, clearly a pair-bonded item, seemed to be outcasts from the main colony. And there was mischief afoot – more than mischief.

Right from the first day that they started to build a nest they were being mobbed by gangs from the main flock. Rowdy threes and fours would fly across at regular intervals to harry them. Initially they surrounded the incipient nest and harangued its builders with aggressively raucous cries, hopping from branch to branch, occasionally diving in and clashing with the builders. Then, when each of my pair flew off to gather sticks, one or more of the gang would follow and mob the poor bird, often causing it to drop its twig. Meanwhile, if they left the nest unattended even for a minute, others of the gang would nip in and dismantle it, skimming back to the main rookery with stolen twigs in their bills.

I watched this going on for days ('Do hurry up and get out of the bath, John'), slowing the nest-building process right down – two twigs forward, one twig back – but never quite defeating my poor outcasts. Long after all the other nests were complete and most of the hens were incubating, my valiant pair was still patching and repairing, still suffering raids from occasional mobsters, until finally the bullies had too many domestic duties of their own to bother. Only then was my pair able to lay eggs and settle to some quieter level of conjugal privacy and isolation.

It was also an interesting observation of human behaviour

to note that when rook domesticity finally won through, Lucy began to take much more interest in the whole drawn-out affair. Our morning bath sessions became punctuated with 'What are they doing now? Have they managed to lay eggs yet? Do you think the chicks have hatched? Oh, I do hope those beastly bullies will keep away.'

They did somehow manage to rear two young, and a year later a second nest was built beside the first, perhaps by one of my pair's young with a new partner, but they were to suffer the same treatment to such an outlandish degree that after a while they gave up and disappeared. A Mafia mob from the main rookery quickly stole all their sticks, dismantled the whole assemblage so that the nest vanished altogether, a thuggish gang retribution as if they had refused to pay their protection dues. This quite upset the normally placid Lucy, whose verdict was immediate and damning: 'Those bullies deserve to be shot.'

This outcast/outlier nest phenomenon is not unknown. It's well documented in the literature, although it seems to be shrouded in myth and folklore. One plausible explanation is that rooks are so obsessively gregarious that they won't allow new nests unless they are very close by. This is all very well, but it doesn't explain why the outcasts should be outcasts in the first place. One frequently cited report claims that following the destruction of an outlier nest the outcast pair were then subjected to a 'rook court' where the elders of the colony sat round in a ring in a field and appeared to be admonishing the demoralised pair in the middle. Hmm, well, I think that may be one for Old Malkie.

Admonished outcasts or not, my pair won. They hung on and raised their brood and to this day the nest is intact, a handsome black blob high in the lime, and I can still lie in my bath and watch them hubbub-ing about their urgent affairs. Whether or not they are now accepted members of the main rookery is unclear. They still draw attention from the mob, but far less aggressively, and for the present the nest remains perhaps not *virgo*, but certainly *intacta*.

★    ★    ★

Before I depart the colourful world of rooks (for now – their story is far from over), I have one more tale to tell. In the 1950s, when I was twelve years old and at a Somerset boarding school, I rescued a fledgling rook that had been storm-gusted from the nest before it could fly. I don't think it was badly hurt, but it sat huddled in the long grass at the foot of a large elm, crying wheezily to its parents high above who probably hadn't noticed one of their brood missing.

I was thrilled. By the age of twelve I had raised (not always successfully) many orphans: squirrels, rabbits, hedgehogs, a whole brood of greenfinches after their mother was snatched by a sparrowhawk, even a fox cub. I caught the genderless rooklet in my hands and carried it home rejoicing. I gave it a suitably sexless name – Squawky. For the rest of that summer term, my last at the school, I was the envy of many boys, who vainly searched the drive avenue of elms for Squawkys of their own.

Squawky never flew and I never knew why. There was

nothing broken, both wings flapped vigorously, and he knew enough about flight to use them for extended flapping lurches from perch to shoulder or head or other convenient landing. Try as I might, I never got him to do more than cross a room. Outside I thrust him up into the air in the hope of teaching him the joy of rapturous flight. He flapped raggedly to the ground twenty yards away where he landed entirely normally, then strutted about looking indignant. I took him back to the avenue to show him the wavering in-and-out flights of his own kind and to listen to their raucous chorale. He would sit on my forearm, head tilting quizzically at the wild birds high above, but with no hint of any inclination to join them. After many fruitless attempts I gave up.

He became my constant companion. During lessons he would sit outside the classroom on a windowsill peering in and occasionally tapping on the glass to attract my attention. Other boys either loved Squawky and followed me enviously about, begging me to let them 'have a go', by which they meant let him sit on their shoulder for a while, or they jealously resented the attention I garnered and sniped at me with snide remarks like 'Serves you right if he craps on your essay.' Even the headmaster revealed tolerant sufferance in his mild but humourless sarcasm, 'Lister-Kaye seems to know nothing about arithmetic but everything about crows.'

At the end of term, and to my utter desolation, on the illogical pretext that because I was moving on to another boarding school I couldn't look after a pet rook, I was not allowed to take Squawky home. A friendly domestic lady called Ruby, who worked in the school kitchens and who for many weeks had offered a clandestine supply of left-over scraps for Squawky, came to my rescue. A gem she truly was. She took pity on me or the rook, or both, and offered to have him. Her farm labourer husband agreed to build an aviary onto their cottage in the village nearby. With a heavy but grateful heart, I delivered the rook into it on my last day.

Life moves on. I have to confess that I never gave Squawky much thought again until one day twenty-two years later I happened to be driving past that Somerset village (the prep school had long since closed) and turned down its only street, trying to remember where precisely Squawky had been housed. I recognised the cottage straight away, unmissable for the spacious wire-netting aviary attached to its gable end. I parked the car and walked up the garden path. To my utter astonishment, I was met by rasping cries from a ragged-looking and extremely ancient rook with an almost bald head. It was Squawky.

He was certainly not beautiful. His naturally featherless cheeks had developed the leathery baldness of a welding glove, a mark of age all rooks over three produce as an adaptive response to habitually piercing the damp soil with their dagger bills in search of leatherjacket grubs. The soiled feathers around the bill simply give up and fail to grow; in the same way some vultures and storks are bald for endlessly thrusting their heads inside rotting carcasses. At nearly twenty-three Squawky's cheeks were huge and as muddy white as a mushroom, made more sinister by the almost total absence of black feathers on his domed skull. He looked like a bad caricature of a vulture with a straight bill or a stork with a short one. But most comical of all were his pantaloons. His feathery trousers, reaching well below his black-scaly knees, were a cross between gamekeepers' plus-fours and the 1930s tennis shorts worn by Indian army colonels.

The kind farm-labourer husband was long departed to build celestial aviaries, and Squawky and the widow Ruby, his almost-stone-deaf, now-in-her-eighties mistress, had lived on in happy andro-corvid companionship for many years. I spent a rapt and nostalgic hour shouting to her so loudly that Squawky, several yards away outside, became agitated and excitedly joined in most of the conversation. Her hearing can't have been so bad because at one point I made the forgivable slip of calling the bird 'my rook'. As quick as a flash the old lady leaned forward and corrected me: 'No, dearie, *my* rook.'

I fed Squawky some porridge and scrambled egg – his favourite dish of more than two decades lovingly prepared by Ruby, which he gobbled noisily and with great vigour, swiping his bill clean on the edge of the bowl when he'd finished. I departed still not quite believing that rooks could live so long.

★ ★ ★

My enthusiasm for rooks has digressed me from what was so extraordinary in November. They should not have been nest-building at all. I didn't know it at the time, but something was upsetting the biorhythms that govern the lives of most of our wildlife, whether visible from my bath or not. The rooks were confused. At first I thought it might be the length of daylight that baffled them, imagining that early November had the same length of day at our latitude as their normal nesting time in February, but I was wrong. There is more than an hour and a half's difference – far too broad a wedge to disorientate an intelligent bird like a rook.

Could the temperature have been the same, triggering some deep genetic impulse to build nests? But, no, the mean temperatures for early November and late February were more than 4° Celsius apart for the previous year. So what had done it? What had brought them to my bathroom window, to dance and haggle through the un-leafing tree tops, to soar and plunge and cry among the striping rays of the lowering sun? Just what else was going on?

# 5

# Prints in the Snow

What freezings I have felt, what dark days seen,
What old December's bareness everywhere!
'Sonnet 97', William Shakespeare

December is winter, no denying it. If wet November winds
pile in, sodden but mild, you can still argue that autumn
lingers on, but not in December. November trails its coat;
December slams the door. And it isn't just the long darkness,
although its melancholy gloom does smother everything,
even hopes and dreams.

It's the shopping list winter brings to our Highland glen
that becomes so inescapable in December, and any of it can
happen at any time: the bone-aching cold, as temperatures
skirt around freezing for days on end, a cold that seems to
penetrate far deeper than that of harder frosts and from
which I can find relief only with a hot bath. Then the unexpected plunge to −15° Celsius of a moonlit night; squalls of
merciless sleet; the mess of slush; black ice bringing sudden,
bruising falls to the unwary; castigating rain; knife-edged
winds from the north and east that slice off your legs at the
knees; the absurdly crimped daylight for any outdoor work.
As our field centre maintenance man, Hugh Bethune, says
of outdoor chores, with characteristically succinct Black Isle

sagacity, 'In December if you don't get it done before lunch, you're buggered!'

Little wonder the badgers stay curled up underground for up to ten days at a stretch. One animal we monitored carefully with stealthcams all winter chose to emerge only as far as the sett entrance, sniff the cold, wet wind and turn back to bed. Even when we put out tempting food for him he would stray only a few feet from the sett to reach it before shuffling back. Yet, for a naturalist, one of the joys of early snows is the chance to read the land and its wildlife in a way you can only dream about until that first tell-tale dusting. Snow brings a new dimension of awareness, a brief window into the other world, the world of animals abroad and of life unseen and uncharted for the rest of the year.

Last night's was well predicted. The council gritter came through in the early morning and did its stuff; well before dawn I could see its amber flashing light on the glen road in the distance. An inch and a half at most – nothing, really – but I couldn't wait to get out. It had fallen wet, not powdery, deep enough to take a full print, and the temperature hovering at zero had just clinched its sharp edges, preventing any melt – perfect tracking snow. It made that rubbery crunch as I trod, packing fast into the tread of my boots.

It is the silence of mornings like this that always grabs me, makes me stand and listen. It is as though the world has stopped spinning for a moment and everything is still. The birds, those few that are left through the cold months, are also silent. I have to stand for several minutes before I hear the thin *seep*-ing of goldcrests high above me in a Douglas fir. Then a cock blackbird comes hurtling through, heading for the bird table. He lands with a chuckle, ebony tail erect and his tangerine bill flaring in the new light, like a struck match.

December is not a month for birds. We have the tits, of course, the busy blues, the bossy greats and the cheeky coals. They all visit the bird feeders and tables together in a flutter of tiny wings, tolerating each other, but only just. Our resident robins come too, prattling and ticking, rather than singing, saving their energy to fight off the cold. The common woodpeckers of the north, the greater spotteds, decked in their livery of black and white and red, like a guided missile, slice through the cold air in an undulating bee-line for the suspended peanut feeder. The woodpeckers always bring a touch of style and regimental sharpness to the group as they cling vertically to the wire. Recently a cock pheasant has been striding in to peck and scratch under the feeders. He doesn't belong here and won't stay long, but his extravagant Oriental glamour makes me smile. I'm not out for the birds this morning. I want to see who else has been calling.

First to the hen run. If we've had visitors in the night it will always be to the hens. Over the years I have found the tracks of just about everything with sharp teeth surrounding the wooden hen-house: foxes, badgers, stoats, pine martens, wildcats, otters, weasels, even mink. It must be exasperating for a hungry predator on a night of stinging cold to know

63

that a hot, delicious dinner is only an inch or two away on the other side of slender boards.

Every once in a while something scores. Usually a pine marten, unless (happily only on rare occasions) one of us forgets to drop the hatch at dusk (Lucy blames me, I her) – then Mr Fox has the time of his life. In the morning headless corpses are strewn all round the paddock, and for weeks afterwards the dogs find straggled hands of feathers, the ragged ends of wings or the odd scaly foot abandoned under dense rhododendrons.

The pine marten is a different matter, harder to keep out and devastating if he gets in. Martens are intelligent, diligent and dextrous. If one chews his way in under the door, squeezing his liquid body through the gap like toothpaste from a tube, the result is mayhem. Once the killing instinct is triggered, and because he can't drag a dead hen out through the hole, he fires his frustration and his ripping canines into every last bird. He becomes a terrorist. Mayhem ensues. To open the door at first light is to view Samson's slaughter of the Philistines. Corpses heaped in every direction. Once it was twenty-seven hens.

There is extra pathos to a murdered hen. It's that pale lower eyelid half eclipsing the eye and the slight gape of the beak that does it; the ignominious end to an undignified existence. The majority of hens live lives of witless desperation in batteries, but Lucy's are the lucky ones, loved and well blessed. A constant cocktail of left-overs from the kitchen is mixed with their corn; let out every morning, tucked up every night, and a half-acre of wormy old paddock to roam and scratch in. But when I'm sent to collect the eggs and I have to sneak my hand in under a hot, fluffy bum, stealing her pride and her only treasures, I feel a clawing sense of guilt, assuaged only by the thought of scrambled egg the colour of dandelions and by convincing myself that the poor bird has neither the sense nor the instinct to comprehend this outrageous exploitation of her most precious assets.

Not so when the pine marten strikes. Even a hen knows a predator when she sees one. Wild Indian jungle fowl, *Gallus gallus*, the progenitor of all domestic chickens, have been dreading predators for something close to a hundred and fifty million years since they emerged in the Jurassic as dinosaurs in feathered disguise. There is nothing we can teach them about fear of predators. In that terrible moment of catatonic panic the hen-house flips in an instant from a sanctuary into a bloody death chamber.

I've never witnessed that panic, but I've heard it. The cacophony of screaming hens woke me and sent me rushing out, pyjamaed, across the yard to do what little I could. Too late. As I opened the door the marten shot out between my legs and vanished into the darkness. It was years ago and I can't remember now how many survived, but only one or two. The rest lay twitching and flapping in the sawdust as if they had been electrocuted.

★　　★　　★

This morning, before the lie-abed sun stirred, I circled the hen-house slowly, carefully placing my feet so as not to blot out the tell-tale prints. The day rose around me, pale and silent. The pine marten had called, all right, all round, up over the nest box lids and onto the felted roof. Searching . . . searching . . . longing for the chink of a gap he could work at – to no avail, I'm glad to report. The prints are immaculate. I can see all five toes and the rosebud curve of the centre pad, claws like punctuation marks dotting each toe. I see where he leaped up onto the nest box lid . . . along it . . . and then long scratches, like etched runes, as he sprang up again, as agile as a squirrel, across the roof.

I try to imagine his every move. I can read the pauses, see the head rise to look around, the front pads pressing further in – martens are as constantly on the *qui vive* as a nervous meerkat. I see where he has risen onto his hind legs, intelligent pointed little face testing the air, his long tail faintly feathering the snow behind him, then bounding on in the sinuous, looping pace that so characterises all martens. I guess at the time spent, probably only a minute and a half, ninety seconds of fiercely focused scrutiny, before he headed off again to check out the next best chance of supper.

A fox has been here too, but earlier, because the marten tracks have crossed on top of the fox's. How much earlier is anyone's guess. I stand and stare. A dog or a vixen? I wonder. The sun is struggling through, glowing in a sea of mist. The morning spreads in front of me like a vision. The snow begins to sparkle, brimming with new light. A hoodie crow comes rowing across the lightening sky, sees me and swerves away. As he goes he calls out, once, twice, three times in a mocking cry, rough-edged with contempt. The fox prints weave a thin line across the lawn, purposeful, but not hurrying. They are bright-rimmed, shining with reflected sun, and dark-shadowed in the sunken pads, bringing them into sharp relief.

He stopped at the base of a large Oriental spruce and scraped at the ground, turning a small stone – a beetle perhaps? Then urinated by lifting a leg – ha! This was a dog fox, not a vixen. He skirted the hen run – tracks now criss-crossed with those of the marten – as I guess he does every night, snow or no snow, so he knows very well that if the hatch is shut it's not his lucky night. So he passed on, across the paddock and over the broken fence, rear pads side by side, pressed deeper as he springs, touching just once with a scuff on the top rail, then onto the old farm road. I curse silently: I have often noticed those scuff marks before, scratches in the lichen and the green *protococcus* algae on the rail, and wondered what had made them. Rooks, I had guessed, wrongly. I should have thought fox: I knew this was his circuit, his private byway. I had often caught a snatch of his vulpine scent, as rich as pickle, just here beside the fence. A thought passes through: perhaps the spurt of effort for springing up releases extra scent, or could it be that, because he is raised as he leaps onto the fence rail, closer to the human nose, he laces another layer of air with molecules of animal musk, an invisible stratum that lingers in the static air, wafting like smoke? Hmm. I had never linked the scent with the scuff marks until now. I set off up the hill, following his trail and feeling a little foolish.

He's not walking; he's trotting in a leisurely but springy pace. His oval pads are evenly spaced and almost in a straight line, but not quite, like the repeating pattern of pansies on a quilt. 'Here he went' is what I see and I must conjure the rest out of familiarity. Out of film and pictures in my head, out of long-ago glimpses, out of chance encounters, out of that electrochemical album in my brain. Images filed away in my pre-frontal cortex, where he is now and where I want to fix him in absolute concentration. But imagination is not enough on its own. Like Ted Hughes's 'The Thought Fox', I want to think fox and think this fox right into my head.

> Cold, delicately as the dark snow
> A fox's nose touches twig, leaf;
> Two eyes serve a movement, that now
> And again now, and now, and now
> Sets neat prints into the snow . . .

For a while he sticks to human paths, the old farm track to the top fields and the moor, as though he is travelling somewhere particular. It's known. I'm sure he does this regularly, relying on opportunism and luck to deliver, or perhaps he's *en route*; perhaps he has somewhere in mind; perhaps to the relative warmth of the pinewood beside the loch where foxes know they will find beetles, where there will be good hunting. Somewhere I can't know; something not my business.

As a teenager in the sixties, I used to turn out, like most country boys, to watch the hounds of the local Seavington Hunt, which met outside the Rose and Crown in the Somerset village near my home. The master and hunt servants in pink jackets with mustard collars, breath pluming from the horses' nostrils on a frosty morning and the hounds milling among the crowd. It was a social convention, a ritual mingling of farmers large and small and their many labourers of those days, of gamekeepers, trappers, landowners and gentry, of unshaven old country yokels in ragged raincoats, leaning on sticks, pipes clenched in their teeth under greasy caps, pork-pie hats or battered brown trilbies, weather-tanned faces all smiling toothily, all amiably chatting, all excited at the prospect of a good day.

Every now and again a hound would stray too far and a whipper-in would call him back, 'Thrasher, git orn in!' Their riders immaculately turned out, handsome, heavy-boned horses with huge glossy flanks champed impatiently at their bits, froth dribbling to the ground. Leather boots and saddles creaked through air thick with the tang of hoof oil, Stockholm tar and the rich stable savoury of fresh horse dung. Steel shoes stamped impatiently as the more excitable horses fidgeted, anxious to be off. 'Steady, Damsel, steady now!'

It was colourful and friendly and had about it an air of old country stability and of things unchanged and unchallenged in a pre-mechanised landscape of ponds and ditches, of hand-laid hedges around small fields and cows still milked by hand. Its people all knew each other and seemed to me to belong to the countryside in those days, to be immersed in it and shaped by it, no one out of place. The master called for 'Hounds please!' The horn sliced through the gossip and, to the clatter of shod hoofs on tarmac, the pack moved off.

I remember leaning on a gate next to an old character in leather gaiters and a tatty serge jacket with a collar ripped to the ticking that might once have been a postal or railway uniform. In silence we watched the horses streaming across a hillside two fields away on the far side of a little valley. We could hear the thin wail of the horn and the belling of hounds somewhere in a deep wooded covert to our left. A shout went up from some foot-followers in the field immediately below us. The fox had broken cover and was streaking across open ground, heading right. I jumped up and made to run off in the direction it was taking.

'Hold 'ard, boy!' the old man called out, waving his pipe and pointing its stem to the field. ''E's comin' back.'

I stopped. 'What d' you mean?' I asked, puzzled.

''E's runnin' up wind to lead 'em on. 'E'll double back in a minute, you'll see. 'E'll come right by 'ere.' He jabbed his pipe at the gate and the lane. I waited and watched. The fox crossed the field and sped on out of sight. Just as I was wishing I had ignored the advice and followed the fox, I glimpsed him again as he turned along a dense thorn hedge, ran swiftly up to the field beside the lane, then turned again downwind, heading back towards our gate. He passed only a few feet away, that fox, a russet streak with a bright white tip to his tail, hearts racing, his and mine, his fired with adrenalin, mine with all the pulsating excitement of the moment. Then he stopped, looked back, black ears tilted to the yelping hounds in the valley below, and silently slid away through the hedge and into the lane. He turned downhill and sped off out of my sight.

That old countryman knew the ways of the hunted fox. Years of watching had taught him what tricks foxes employ when pressed: doubling back, crossing water to diffuse scent, climbing haystacks, even jumping onto the back of moving farm trailers unbeknown to the tractor driver – the tales are endless and often tall. It's how they came to earn the reputation of sly and cunning. I was glad to learn from him and the fox that day.

It's easy to say, 'I know the ways of the fox. I know what he'll do.' The old man did know: he knew exactly what the fox was likely to do because he'd seen it all so many times before. I respected him then and I respect him now, but it would be wrong to suggest he knew the natural history of the fox. We are so often arrogant in our androcentric analysis of the world around us. What we see we think we understand and we seldom give a thought for what we don't see. We piece together our glimpses, like a jigsaw cut to fit the image of our own perceptions. Then we give it a name – sly or cunning – and it sticks.

In my lifetime science has come barrelling in, grabbed the knowledge and taken over the name-giving. Our lives have moved away from the farm gate and the hedge. 'Field' wisdom has given way to 'field guide' wisdom. We look it up or we Google it, blindly accepting the one-dimensional Wiki-wisdom as gospel and all we need to know. Oh, yes, they mate in January, gestation is seven and a half weeks and they have an average of five young, called cubs, in a burrow known as an earth. They have a weight and a length nose to tail, a range and a territory and a distribution map. They're omnivorous or carnivorous or dimorphic or polygamous or double-brooded or something-or-other else. It's all very matter-of-fact and a bit smug, but not how the fox sees it – not at all.

Every once in a while I've come across a naturalist who really does *know* at a level that defies science, often dismissed as 'amateur' or 'circumstantial evidence'. The late Eric Ashby, who lived in the New Forest and captured astonishing (for the 1960s) film footage of foxes, badgers, hares and deer, was one of those. He was a shy man with a private passion for wildlife. I met him only once. I went to interview him for a magazine article and walked through the forest with him for a couple of hours one afternoon. He impressed me in a way I have never forgotten. He possessed an almost palpable whole-awareness of his surroundings as though he had become part of the woods, or the woods had somehow become absorbed into his bloodstream. His outstanding humility and modesty were also the characteristics of his work as a naturalist. 'Never presume anything,' he told me, with a wry smile. 'You'll almost always be wrong.'

Eric gleaned his knowledge by dogged legwork and with the patience of a gravestone. If it needed a hundred hours of silent observation to find something out, then a hundred hours he'd give it. Another of these was the late Eileen Soper, wildlife artist and author of several wildlife books, charmingly illustrated with her own drawings. She took me badger-watching when I was a schoolboy and introduced me to what I can only describe as another way of being human.

As we approached the setts in the dusk she seemed to slough off her human-ness and transmogrify into something more than half wild. I couldn't understand how she sat so still. She denied cold and rain, she ignored itches – a gnat landing on her nose – she seemed to become part of the wood herself, part of the tree, the soil, the still evening air. She had developed the discipline and serenity of a Buddhist monk and the concentration of a hypnotist. Little wonder the badgers accepted her so unconditionally. Cubs took biscuits from her hand; adults sniffed at her legs and set scent on her shoes – the ultimate acceptance of a wild badger – claiming her as their own. It was Eileen who wrote in one of her books, 'I think badger-watchers are not entirely human.'

\*     \*     \*

The tracks stop and I stop with them. Has my fox plucked a sound from the night air into those black, A-frame, ever-swivelling sensors? Snatched a molecule of scent and cradled it in olfactory awareness? Or is it a combination of senses working together? One front pad has swivelled slightly to the right. I think he's looking and listening to the right, and his prints are pressed deeper and smudged, as though they have shifted fractionally, as if he was about to move and thought better of it. For a moment we are one, the fox and I, sharing the same chill oxygen, senses straining, poised, expectant.

He is still on the farm track, but right beside the verge of long, ragged grass and frost-killed weeds. Then he moves on, slowly, just a few short paces . . . two . . . three . . . four . . . and stops again, closer now to the verge. I try to guess how long he stood there. The pads are pressed home and have crumbled slightly at the edges from the warmth of his feet. I think he was rigid, frozen into listening mode, taut as a piano wire, and not just for a few seconds.

On again, but it's all different. The prints are bunched up, short and staccato. I can't decide whether he is stalking because he's seen something or just leoparding forward, a few inches at a time. Then it's all clear: the story is plain, there for the deciphering, like suddenly discovering a new panel of hieroglyphics on an ancient tomb, revealing everything. My pulse quickens. I'm with him, eyes unpicking the signals, brain flicking through a scrapbook of images, conjuring new ones. Because I've seen it on film, in photographs and witnessed it myself through binoculars, this little bit of the fox I do know. Without that knowledge the tracks would be an incomprehensible mess, but I can match the mess to the image and paint a masterpiece in my head.

It was hearing, I'm sure. He first picked up the rustling through frosted stems a few paces back down the track. That's why he stopped, to listen. He knew it was a mouse or a vole and his taut, pointed ears, like radar scanners, and his nose focused in together, collecting data, building the image and the range. In snow, small mammals have to tunnel around beneath the surface to feed, probably oblivious to any dangers that may be lurking above. Then he stalked, my fox – five short, finely placed steps, one by silent one – to the edge of the grass. He paused again, head cocked, ears trained down, wet nostrils quivering wide, eyes burning into a patch of snow half right and a foot or two into the verge.

I think he stood poised there for several seconds until, with a springing pounce, his strong back legs powered him up in an arcing curve to land exactly where he knew his prey was, front pads both pounding together to dash the small mammal into confusion, instantly followed by the sharp snout, probing deep into the frosty mat of the grass.

It didn't quite end there. He caught that wood mouse or, more likely because of the grassy habitat, a field vole (*Microtus agrestis*), and flicked it up with his teeth to get it clear of the grass. Five strands of torn yellow grass lay on the snow as though he had shaken them from his mouth. The vole landed a foot away, almost certainly mortally injured, and he snapped it up again, leaving only a slight imprint such as you might make with two fingers pressed gently in.

My fox has wafted through our winter landscape unaware that he was leaving his signature for anyone who cared to read it. That I did is my route to him and his world. It is a world I cannot join or ever hope to understand fully, but it is one that delivers up a particular and private fulfilment. He has been here: bright-eyed, alert, as taut as a bow-string, fluid and sensuous, luminous with heat and life. I have followed: rapt, absorbent, charged, intent. Our lives have crossed and I am the happier for it. I see the fox as a survivor, a sublime embodiment of all the things I love so much about nature: the necessity, the opportunism, the independence of spirit, the wholeness of being, the absolute distillation of wildness. My fox went on. I turned back to the house to get on with being human again.

# 6

# A Swan for Christmas

Some full-breasted swan
That, fluting a wild carol ere her death,
Ruffles her pure cold plume, and takes the flood
With swarthy webs.

'The Passing of Arthur',
Alfred, Lord Tennyson


. . . as I have seen a swan
With bootless labour swim against the tide
And spend her strength with over-matching waves.

*King Henry VI*, Part 3, Act 1, scene iv,
William Shakespeare


Medieval kings loved to eat swans. Roast swan is widely recorded as a speciality that was laid on for the wedding feasts, banquets and royal celebrations of Merrie England. I have tried it a few times, and won't bother again. They must have had culinary skills I lack and, I suspect, husbandry secrets I don't care to think about.

We have two swans in the Highlands: the large archetypal mute swans of *Swan Lake* and which grace calendar pages, swans we all know from city lakes and rivers, which have virtually no fear of human beings, and we have the slightly smaller and, to my mind, far more refined, straight-necked whooper swans that overwinter here and migrate to the Arctic to breed.

Our whoopers arrive here with the winter. They come later than the autumn flocks of grey geese and seem to haul winter along behind them. They migrate in from Iceland and Arctic Scandinavia in small family groups. Every year we expect to have between ten and twenty in the valley. They like the sheltered lochs that are slow to freeze and they will stay on the open water of the Beauly River and its oxbow lakes when the ice comes. In extreme frost – I have seen the river freeze over only a few times in my forty years – they repair to the tidal shallows of the east coast, where I have occasionally seen whoopers gathered in huge flocks.

A few of them die here every winter. Electricity distribution lines criss-cross the glen and the river in several places. Flying swans – both the delicate whoopers and the much heavier resident mutes – spot the thin wire too late. They collide and it kills them; if not straight away, then slowly in the agony of a broken wing and starvation. I am not emotional about the death of wildlife; it's a fact of everyday wildness to which I am entirely reconciled. But to see a glowing white swan flapping in helpless circles beneath the wires never fails to anger me. Over the years I have braced myself to despatch several and I've found the fox-strewn feathers of many more. In one dreadful event a few years ago six whoopers crashed into the wires together at the spot where they cross the river fields only half a mile from my home. Two were instantly electrocuted, one cygnet died of a broken neck and the other three suffered broken wings.

Once or twice I have taken a freshly dead carcass and tried to cook it – not to be recommended. I have come to the conclusion that the swans of medieval feasts cannot have been of the migratory ilk: they must have been resident mute swans, and were most likely fattened up for royal fare. The whoopers I have sampled have been lean, stringy and as chewy as old hemp rope. I have even tried carefully removing only the breast meat and casseroling it slowly in a low oven, but with little improvement. Those breast muscles have just powered the huge birds for many hundreds of miles of migration. Swan is no longer on my menu.

Whooper swans fly and feed by night and day. As they fly they call to each other, which is how they arrived at their onomatopoeic name. It is a soft-edged bugling phonetically described as a whoop, pitched like a B♭ flugelhorn, with a fatter, mellower tone closer to that of a French horn than a trumpet or military bugle. Typically the call repeats itself three or four times, a single unhurried note with an inaudible snatch of breath between each one. When six or seven birds are flying together in close formation, wings almost touching, their soft flugelings overlap in a rare and disturbing music that can be heard for miles.

If they leave the river at night and head up over the forest to our little eight-acre loch, they have to pass within a few hundred yards of my bedroom window. I hear them far off and I'm out of bed in a flash. In bright moonlight they gleam like mercury as they pass.

Two weeks before Christmas I heard them clearly, the sound pealing through the damp, cold air, like a call to arms. I couldn't wait for morning – dawn frustratingly late at 8.40 forty. I hurried up the hill, easing back to stealth as I topped the rise at the dam. The loch sits in a hollow surrounded by dark pine forest with a broad marsh at the south-western shore, open moorland beyond. There they were, seven of them, glowing like virgin brides at the far end of the loch. They were feeding in the shallows, probing and sifting the mire for their favourite mix of aquatic weeds and roots – a sort of peaty vichyssoise. Their heads rose and fell as they dabbled, and every few minutes they would flute to each other in intimate, barely audible hoots, quite distinct from their flight calls.

I watched them on and off for four days. Whenever I needed to get out of the house I headed uphill to the loch. Sometimes they were out of the water in the marsh, standing or walking freely, their necks immediately upright if they saw me, bright nares shining daffodil yellow in the winter sun. Three were cygnets, unmistakably grey and without the hallmark yellow bills that make them so distinct from mute swans. Hatched in the Lapland or Iceland summer, this was their first migration south, a journey that would hopefully be repeated many times.

On the fifth day I arrived just in time to see them go. I stood silently among the birches at the dam. Very slowly they paddled line-abreast down the loch towards me, long necks as straight as walking sticks. They seemed uneasy, no doubt very well aware that human presence had been seen there every day. Their muted calls were edgy and nervous. Heads swivelled anxiously. As they approached the dam one mature bird bugled loudly, as if giving a signal. As one they turned and thrashed their long white wings against the dark water, rising up from the surface and paddling furiously into a diagonal take-off down the full length of the loch towards the marsh. The morning air rang with the loud flaying of fourteen powerful wings and feet; the surface was momentarily whipped into seven long trails of creamy foam.

Six swans lifted weightily into the cold, misty air. They cleared the marsh by only a few feet and banked away south, still rising, over the heather moorland and the crowns of dark pines until they were clear of the hills. The seventh bird failed to gain enough height. It was forced to abort its take-off and crashed clumsily into the marsh. Its companions circled overhead. The air rang with their throbbing wingsong; their flugeling calls now rimmed with anxiety echoed loudly from the forest fringe. They circled twice, each time higher, but constantly calling out to their fallen friend. Then they lifted away over the forest and were gone. The last I saw of them was a silhouetted chevron against paler clouds, high above the pines heading away towards the river in the valley far below.

The fallen bird paddled urgently back to the dam. A bow wave flowed out from its breast and into a spreading wake behind. It turned to try again. This time it seemed to rise well. By halfway down the loch it was clear of the water, only the downdraught from its wing tips rippling the surface. But it couldn't seem to gain any more lift. As it neared the marsh it lost its nerve and aborted again, thrusting its black feet forward, emergency brakes furrowing the surface as it crashed down in an undignified tangle of wings and water.

I watched it try twice more, but with decreasing success. The last attempt was half-hearted. It seemed to have realised it was too weak to lift off. It cried out. Now the soft fluge-ling I love so much was keened with stress. The loch fell silent. I retreated. Perhaps if it rested it would get off in an hour or two.

But it didn't.

I went back several times each day for the next two days. The swan had taken up a position on the edge of the marsh where it stood looking lost and forlorn. It was sporadically feeding – or, at least, going through the motions of feeding. I have lived at Aigas long enough to know that our loch offers very limited food for water birds in winter. Mallard come and go, but never stay long. The water is too acid and too peaty and it freezes regularly, sometimes for long periods and to such a depth of ice that we can skate safely. I could see that my swan had given up trying. I decided to act.

I don't normally interfere with nature. On many occasions I have been in a position to frighten away a predator and save a life, a sparrowhawk hauling down a hapless blackbird or chaffinch or hooded crows stealing chicks from a robin's nest, but the predators have to live too and I do not like playing God. Anyway, Darwin's mantra echoes constantly in my head: 'It is the fittest that survive.'

Yet this seemed to me to be different. I love whooper swans and it would have distressed me deeply to watch it starve. But I also felt that there was an element of rotten luck in the bird's plight, something not its fault, like tawny owls that see a chimney and decide to explore it as a nest hole, only to find themselves sitting in a fireplace, trapped in an empty bedroom, unable to fly back up the chimney, doomed to starvation. My swan had flown in with its healthy family companions. It didn't know it lacked the strength to get off again until it tried, and by then it was too late. I was sure there was insufficient natural feed in the loch to build it up again.

My best guess is that migration had taken too much out of it. Perhaps it was an older bird – its pure white plumage and bright yellow bill markings told me it was certainly mature. Perhaps they'd had to battle against strong head winds. Perhaps the subtle shifts in our winter weather patterns had pushed them off course, making the journey longer and more arduous than usual. Perhaps my swan was carrying a parasite burden or some other ailment. I have no way of knowing – to me, it was just a sad, knackered swan and I knew very well that nature gives no quarter. I walked slowly back to the house. We feed the birds on our bird table every day. Why should the poor swan be different? Besides, it was nearly Christmas. I decided to feed it.

I stole a bucketful of mixed corn – wheat, barley and chopped maize – from Lucy's chicken-feed bins and spread it in generous handfuls along the edge of the marsh. The swan backed off to the middle of the loch and eyed me warily. I went away. A few hours later I sneaked back to the birches and watched through binoculars. It was feeding, head down in the rushes exactly where I had put the corn. So were six greedy mallard.

Word got out. Over the next week the mallard numbers increased dramatically. I put a bucketful of corn out every day to ensure that there was always enough for my swan. At one point there were sixteen mallard guzzling there. I could hardly blame them: they are real survivors. But my swan was feeding too and by now it had a permanently bulging crop at the base of its neck. Its plumage shone like fresh snow. It looked well.

After ten days I had begun to wonder if it would ever be able to leave. That clear frosty morning I walked up the hill with my bucket, the Jack Russells dashing about at my feet. I saw no need for stealth or caution: the swan was always there at the marsh. At the dam I stood and scoured the entire loch now sealed with a skim of ice. No swan. I walked round the loch searching, praying I wouldn't find a swan corpse. No swan. It had gone. I walked up the moorland through the deep heather in case it had tried to walk out and to reassure myself that it could never have taken off from there. No swan. I went back to the marsh. Not a sign except for regular extrusions of very healthy-looking green dung and a few preened feathers where it had roosted at the water's edge.

My swan had flown away.

Was it the plunging temperature and the ice forming around it that had triggered its move? Did it know instinctively that if the ice thickened it would be stuck for good? Or had my high-quality feed restored its confidence as well as its strength? I would never know.

Later that day I drove slowly down the valley, eyeing the river wherever I could get a good view through the trees. There were a few places I knew the whoopers liked to hang out – an oxbow lake and a stagnant meander with a grassy bay about three miles upstream. I parked the car and walked across a rough croft meadow crisp with rime. As I neared the riverbank I heard the clear ringing call of whoopers coming from just beyond my view in that very bay. Then the thrashing wind-throb of multiple feet and wings. A line of lashing white wings whirled past me and away down the river. I watched them rise majestically into a bright winter sky of stabbing blue. Silver-shouldered they banked in a broad circle above the trees and headed back upriver over my head. They were in a shallow V, four on one side, three on the other, necks outstretched, wings powering in a unison of perfect timing. Seven glorious whoopers, wild and free. In seconds they were gone from my view, but their flugel-horns rang out loud and clear.

# 7

# The Day the Sun Stands Still

> The night is darkening round me,
> The wild winds coldly blow;
> But a tyrant spell has bound me,
> And I cannot, cannot go.
>
> The giant trees are bending
> Their bare boughs weighed with snow;
> The storm is fast descending,
> And yet I cannot go.
>
> Emily Brontë (1818–48)

Some four or five thousand years ago, in the wind-scoured yet sandstone-fertile archipelago of Orkney, an individual, or perhaps a group (a committee?) of the nameless, raceless people we have clumsily branded Neolithic or late Stone Age sat round the fire and hatched a plan.

It was probably clear that their chieftain was not long for this world. Perhaps he had been a bit of a hero, no doubt a thoroughly good bloke. He'd probably sired fine sons, won battles, lopped off a few truculent heads and kept the local raiders out. He might even have headed up a bit of a dynasty. In any event, they thought he deserved a special tomb.

Well, they did him proud. Thankfully, the result of their deliberations and their remarkable skills, the chambered cairn of Maeshowe is with us today more or less intact. It is thoughtfully constructed, with a low entrance tunnel and a square central room beneath a vaulted ceiling and three much smaller chambers off – an edifice of refinement and beauty, a result to be proud of. Historic Scotland, the government agency responsible for its upkeep, describes it as one of the finest architectural achievements of prehistoric Europe. Others call it a 'Neolithic cathedral' and attest that the stone masonry involving individual slabs weighing up to three tons each would seriously challenge today's masonry skills. Luckily they surrounded it with a large circular ditch; it is the carbon-dated peat from the bottom of that ditch which gives us the near-as-dammit accurate date of 2750 BC.

For me, by far the most galvanising aspect of Maeshowe is that the entrance tunnel is precisely aligned with the setting sun on the shortest day of the year – the winter solstice. Exactly similar solar alignment can be found at Stonehenge or New Grange in Ireland, or in Egypt at the temple complex of Karnak on the Nile, built in the pharaonic reign of Senusret I (1971–26 BC). It is present, too, in China's winter season, when the dark *yin* is exactly balanced with the light *yang*. All these and many more ancient cultures, monuments and traditions pay homage to the winter solstice, 21–22 December, as an awesome, mysterious and powerful phenomenon of prodigious ritual or religious significance.

I have been to Maeshowe many times and I always come

away feeling I am missing something really important that they knew; something of the gut, honoured and believed as a life force; some almost palpable otherness – Emily Brontë's 'tyrant spell' – which may have brightly coloured and reassured their lives. What was it that required them to position the whole splendid edifice so that the last rays of the setting sun pierced the darkness of the tomb on Orkney's shortest day, the darkest moment of the northern calendar, flooding the long entrance passage and the back wall of the spacious interior with golden light? We know it as the winter solstice, direct from its Latin derivation, the day when the sun stands still.

It is the moment of rebirth, of the beginning of a new solar year, the sun's rising again, every day inching higher in the sky, bringing with it (in due time) the spring and the revival of growth and opportunity. Hardly surprising, then, that whoever they were, they should have seen it as such an important event. Perhaps they even believed that rolling back the large entrance stone, allowing that spiritually charged light to flood in, would also aid the rebirth of their dead into another life.

Much later, we know from the Orkneyinga Saga, the tomb was raided and probably looted by Vikings under the leadership of Earl (Yarl) Rögnvald and his crusaders on their way to Constantinople in 1153. They left their signatures and explicit graffiti etched in runes on the interior walls. At that moment they seem to have had other things on their minds; the significance of the building to the winter solstice was probably lost on them, but in their own culture it would nevertheless have been as important in their lives as the Norse festival of Yuletide.

They were warriors, fighting men more interested in women than the calendar. Their observations are just what you might expect of such men – although some are rather touching. 'Ingigerth is the most beautiful of all women' and 'Ingebjork the fair widow – many a woman has walked stooping in here a very showy person' signed by 'Erlingr'. These endearments are somewhat sullied by 'Thorni fucked' while 'Helgi carved', an insight studiously omitted from the Orkney guide books.

Now in disguise, in our own confused cultural tradition the winter solstice survives obliquely in the form of Yuletide, Yule being the old Norse month of ýlir, or *jol*, which we celebrate as the twelve days of Christmas. In ancient Norse tradition everyone stopped work and took some time off to give the new solar year a chance to recover and fire itself up.

What particularly grips me about these seemingly obscure connections is that they are a very good illustration of how far we have removed ourselves from the seasons and the constantly turning wheel of nature that has governed human lives ever since we strode out from the primeval forest. To our infinite loss, the materialist vortex of modernity has sucked us away from these ancestral influences, so much so that it is hard now to imagine just what their meaning was, or how important they were to our predecessors, whose lives were lived very much at the mercy of what was often a dangerous and hostile environment.

For many millennia in the accentuated seasons of the northern hemisphere, human survival depended upon the success or failure of harvests. After a bad harvest it must have been deeply worrying – not to say frightening – to witness every autumn the sun slipping lower and lower in the sky, knowing that nothing would grow again for many months. Vegetation died away, offering nothing. Lakes and streams iced over, rendering fishing difficult or impossible, mammals vanished into hibernation and most birds migrated south. The days grew ever darker and colder. Then, at last, came the solstice: the moment in the year when, regardless of the chill and the gloom, everything started up again, even though there would still be many weeks of winter to endure.

Throughout the northern hemisphere mean winter temperatures continue to fall until mid-January because of the angle of tilt of the Earth's axis to the sun. Only as the angle steepens does the vital absorption of solar energy take effect. Despite this, the sense of relief at seeing the sun climb higher and higher every day surely made this a moment for great rejoicing.

The pagan celebration of Yule was so powerful and widespread across the known world that with an if-you-can't-beat-'em-join-'em twist of pragmatism, early Christians reluctantly pitched in, perhaps partly to make Christianity more acceptable to a wider audience. After endless pious debate, and quite possibly glimpsing the recruitment potential, in AD 350 Pope Julius I (now St Julius) conveniently agreed to shift the hotly contested birth of Christ (Christ's Mass) from the best contemporary scholars' historical and astronomical calculation of 6 February, 6 BC to 25 December, a shifting of the goal posts that was nothing if not expedient and could probably only have been achieved by a pope. Even so, the move was highly controversial and wouldn't be fully adopted by the wider Christian Church for many decades. In his own words, the cantankerous Atticus, the fifth-century Archbishop of Constantinople, accepted it only because it allowed him to celebrate Christ's birthday undisturbed while the 'heathens were busy with profane celebrations of their own'.

Pope Julius probably didn't fully realise what a flash of accidental genius it would turn out to be. It was a master-stroke, a cunning twist of calendric doctrine that would hijack so many pagan festivities right across the non-Christian world and smear them seamlessly into the Christian liturgical cycle, as if they had been there all along, thus catapulting Christianity into the vanguard of popular religious appeal.

The logic for this canonical legerdemain was undeniable. No festival to celebrate the birth of Christ had existed before the fourth century, whereas the Romans had long been honouring the Mithraic festival of the winter solstice, held, interestingly, on their 25 December, which coincided exactly with the 21 December of the Gregorian calendar. The Persians called theirs the 'Birthday of the Unconquered Sun'. Norse culture celebrated the birth of their god Freyr, god of sunshine and weather (among many other burdensome responsibilities, such as potency and virility) at the solstice; and even more conveniently for evangelising Christians, the unruly Celts and many other pagan cultures celebrated the solstice as the rebirth of the sun, which, with uncanny seren-dipity, they knew as the 'Birth of the Divine Child'.

Christmas quickly caught on, but the ancient pagan Yuletide connections with Christmas by no means ended there. Yule festivities essentially celebrated the death of the solar year and the birth of the new, the swerve away from darkness and the blessed beginning of the return to light. Long before Christianity claimed it, the symbolic selection and harvesting of a sacrificial living tree was also an impor-tant ritual found in many pagan cultures. The only green trees in winter were the evergreen conifers, nowadays, of course, the Christmas tree. Among the Celtic peoples of northern Europe, evergreens – yews, pines and spruces – were widely celebrated as sacred because they retained life and vigour when everything else died away during the bitter cold. Druids made processions into the forests to pay homage to the renewed life the conifers symbolised. The Roman priests also cut sacred pines, decorated them and carried them into their temples as an offering.

More than this, it was customary to perform other pagan celebration rites that have been subsumed into the Christmas story and are easily recognisable today: bearing gifts for gods (the three kings) as a way of ensuring the return of longer, warmer days and placing them as offerings under the tree; decorating the Yule tree with ornaments representing fruits, nuts and berries was to ensure survival through winter and the return of spring; the handing out of specially prepared confections and cakes (Christmas cake and pudding, mince pies); wassailing or singing carols from household to household; abstaining from hunting and fishing (a holiday) for the twelve days of Yule; and the burning of the Yule log, still widely practised in many European countries.

★   ★   ★

Our big, rumbustious family merrily shrugs off the deception and joins in with the festivities, like everyone else. Throughout all the growing-up years, rushing off into the woods to choose a tree was an essential forerunner to the whole deal, and it was fun. I remember our teenagers almost fighting to perform the deed – 'It's my turn, you did it last year!' – then suffering the taunts from those left out: 'It's too big. You won't get it in the door'; 'That scrubby thing won't do. Go and get a better one!'; 'Is that the best you could find?' and so on, all of which assured me that the ritual significance of the tree to the whole festival of Christmas was still alive and sprouting.

Yet for all the parallels of our modern Christmas festival with the ancient past, never once have I heard anyone make reference to the winter solstice. We have lost it, and I am sad about that. It has gone the way the British harvest festival is rapidly heading. Gone are the days when whole agricultural communities, entire villages and towns viewed their harvest festival in church as a highpoint of their year. Aisles and altars overflowed with produce: baskets of apples, pears and plums, cabbages, eggs, leeks and onions, potatoes, swedes and turnips, marrows and pumpkins cluttering the communion rail; urns of grain, stooks of corn and bales of hay adorned the chancel steps and decorous loaves of specially baked bread rimmed the pulpits, all punctuated with home-produced Kilner jars of plums, gooseberries and other colourful preserves, and cloth-topped jars of jams, pickles and chutneys. Herbaceous flowers and colourful foliage adorned the few remaining spaces. 'We plough the fields and scatter . . .' reverberated through ancient hammer-beam roofs and across graveyards the length and breadth of the land. The shrinking congregations of today have lost their connection with the soil and as a consequence such festivals as are still observed are a lame parody of their former agricultural bounty.

This year, alas, the Aigas solstice was a flop and my plans to revive paganism with a cosy sunset party of mulled claret at the loch with my home-coming family came to naught. Thick cloud and no sun at all. 'The storm is fast descending.' It rained viciously all day on the 20th and 21st, and all that night, icy and driven by a wind possessed. The morning of the 22nd revealed the valley awash; the burn was in roaring spate, like a train that never passed, and the low-lying fields had been gobbled up by the river as if they had never existed. When, at last, on the 23rd the storm abated, the clouds thinned and a lame sun limped briefly into view, the mood had passed. It was too late and too underwhelming to celebrate anything.

I turned in for bed that night subdued, wondering what, precisely, we had missed. Wasn't there some faint echo of biorhythmic memory locked into our genes? Shouldn't I have felt some inner awakening, a frisson from the tyrant spell of those ancient ghosts? Shouldn't the passing of the sun's nadir have aroused my winter spirits? Fired me up? Perhaps you've got to be there and witness it first hand to get the proper message, like standing in front of some exquisite cave painting, telling as much of man as of beast and leaving us in awe of both.

My brooding was premature. Our loyal and resident tawny owls rescued me from the doldrums. My habit of sleeping with one ear cocked to the window beside me, flung wide regardless of the weather, has long been a means of keeping me in touch with the outside world. December into January is an important moment for tawnies. The adult birds are busy defending their territories from adolescent incomers. On still nights the air rings with echoing calls as they battle for space. For me that night the hooting, shrieking and yelling calls of the owls around us were an important return to base. I was back in touch with the wild world I love. I fell asleep thanking the owls and longing to get out there as soon as I could.

With my two Jack Russells, Nip and Tuck, I was up and out early on the 24th. The dawn was cool and clear. The wind had vanished and the floods were seeping away. The rain threat had been displaced by that of Christmas Eve and my lifelong unpreparedness and inability to match up to expectations, a failing I've never managed to crack or to conceal. The very thought seemed to be dragging me away from the whole prospect of the holiday's overblown materialist imperatives. I decided to head off up the hill for a proper walk.

Forty minutes later I puffed and panted up the steep heather slope to our own archaeological high point at seven hundred feet on the glen's rim, an Iron Age fort – now just a pile of stones – overlooking the Beauly River and the snaking glacial valley of Strathglass far below. My timing was immaculate.

Like molten gold from a crucible, the first touch of sun spilled in from the east, from the glistening horizon of the Moray Firth, so bright that I couldn't look at it, flooding its winter fire up the river, right past me and on up the valley. The river trailed below me, like a silk pashmina thrown down by an untidy teenager. Strands of mist over the water were fired with yellow flame, as though part of some mysterious ritual immolation. The new-born light raked the steep glen sides, floodlighting every rocky prominence and daubing deep craters of black shadow so that the familiar shape of the land vanished before my eyes. I was in a wonderland, strange to me and a little unnerving. The dogs sat uncharacteristically silent at my feet, noses lifting to test the air, but stilled as though they, too, could sense the moment.

Unaware of our presence above him, a roe buck was slowly picking his way up the slope in front of me. He was out of the dogs' sight and I stood still, despite being silhouetted against the western sky. I hoped he would keep on coming. Dense broom and gorse crowded the south-facing slope and I lost him in it for several minutes. I was about to turn for home when he reappeared, much closer now and to my right, still heading up. There was no wind.

I could see that he was beautiful, not a bit scrawny as winter roe can sometimes appear, but refined and shapely, the taut musculature beneath awarding body and form to his winter fur, as soft and uniform grey as a Lifeguard's greatcoat. His nose was jet black and a bright white gorget stood out from his throat, like a mayor's badge of rank. He had cast his short, spiky antlers back in October and the new set was growing under dense furry velvet, liquid bone oozing up day by day to be hard and ready by April. They were well on, like the stumpy horns of a giraffe, the spiky tines still fully to form. He radiated quality. He had entered the winter well, with fat rounding his shoulder blades and flanks. Even if it proved to be hard weather for the next two months, he would emerge fit and strong at the end of it, well placed to begin the long build-up to the July rut.

He wasn't just beautiful – he also knew it. He was idly browsing on broom and bramble shoots, plucking them with the insouciant air of a narcissistic aesthete in sharp little flicks of the head. Every few moments he would stop chewing, lift his head and look around with a studied pose of self-belief. There was no hint of alarm or even wariness, just a haughty and quizzical exploration of his domain, perhaps to see if any other buck had dared trespass on his patch. As he did so, his raised head, in perfect profile, was as elegantly statuesque as one of those expensive life-size bronzes to be seen in sporting galleries.

A rag of cloud slid across the sun, dulling its fire for a moment. I looked down at the glen and the river fields and they were there again, as they always had been, familiar and predictable. When I looked up my roe buck was only a few yards away. He had risen to a small rocky spur at the same level as me and the dogs. He had seen me, but hadn't yet identified me as human. His head was up and he was delicately testing the air for scent. Black nostrils twitched and his ears swivelled. As is so often the case with deer, he needed the confirmation of scent to believe what he was seeing. He was staring straight at me. Our eyes collided in a silent, slow-motion crash. He was magnificent. It was a stretched, frozen moment of gripped breath and a riveted stare, impaling him and willing him to stay. Just then the low sun punched through the cloud in a fury of dazzling fire, instantly turning my roe buck and the rock he stood upon not to bronze but to the purest, gleaming gold. It was as though someone had stolen him from Tutankhamen's tomb and planted him on that rock, like a totemic effigy atop an outrageously ostentatious sarcophagus.

Here was my Maeshowe moment, my witness to rebirth and the beginning of the new solar year, the sun's gilded rising bringing the renewal of life, growth, opportunity and the spiritual fillip I had sought.

I was transfixed and the dogs never moved. We stared at each other, that ormolu roe buck and I, for several long, exaggerated seconds before he silently turned and slipped away into the thicket behind him. I stood gazing blankly at the empty rock as if by doing so I could conjure him up again. I waited, expecting to hear him crash away through the undergrowth, as roe deer so often do when they are disturbed, but nothing came. Just the empty silence of the morning. It was as though he had never existed.

My failed winter-solstice party now seemed irrelevant. I

might have missed the moment of the sun's absolute stasis, but for those few seconds a shared fusion of renewed life and vigour had burned in me and the buck. I whistled to the dogs to follow and began the slow, slippery descent to the moor. I think I had begun to understand what the architects of Maeshowe had meant.

# 8

# The Gods of High Places

Did ever raven sing so like a lark,
That gives sweet tidings of the sun's uprise?
*Titus Andronicus*, Act III, scene i,
William Shakespeare

There is nothing dull about a raven. As glossy as a midnight puddle, bigger than a buzzard, with a bill like a poleaxe and the eyes of an eagle, its brain is as sharp and quick as a whiplash. Surfing the high mountain winds, ravens tumble with the ease and grace of trapeze artists, and their *basso profondo* calls are sonorous, rich and resonant, gifting portent to the solemn gods of high places. Ravens surround us at Aigas, and they nest early.

Yesterday, a puzzling January day so gentled by a southerly breeze streaming to us from the Azores that it could easily have been April, I sauntered the half-mile to where the road lifts and snakes east, then veers north high above the river to look down into the black waters of the Aigas gorge, most of which is invisible to the casual passer-by sealed in his car. A day so beguiling under the cool winter sun that great tits began sawing and dunnocks bubbled and trilled from the roadside broom thickets. I wanted to see if the ravens were attending their habitual nest site on a vertical cliff over-hanging the satanic flow of the Beauly River.

They weren't, although a faint 'cronk' from somewhere high above and beyond the forested horizon echoed back at me from the rock walls. I hadn't expected them to be at the nest site so early in the year, but because that seduc-tive airstream had brought the rooks back to their nests for an hour or two before vanishing again, it got me thinking of crows in general and climate change in partic-ular.

Attempting to draw conclusions about aberrations in climate from one or two odd incidents is risky and always bound to be proved wrong when suddenly everything happens in reverse. It is also unwise to work from the premise of any 'norm'. What defines normal weather, and when did it become normal? Is a winter bound to be defined by cold and snow? Clearly not, since Britain and many other parts of northern Europe have experienced mild, wet winters off and on for decades. And yet most careful observers are convinced that our climate is changing. All I can do, trapped in our Highland glen, is to watch and monitor the common standards of climate, temperature, precipitation and wind speed, and do my best to work out the impact these fluctu-ating parameters have on the wildlife around us. I thought the ravens might throw some light on this conundrum.

Ravens are always the first to nest every year – nests built in early February, eggs laid towards the end of the month – but if the weather is clement our gorge pair often spend a few late-January days repairing the twiggy stack, now a yard high, that they have used for the last decade. The Aigas gorge is a perfect site for raising their brood of greedy, belly-bulging, reptilian fledglings. (As I write this, I am struck by an irresistible word-play: ravens nest in the Aigas gorge; ravens gorge in the Aigas nest.)

The valley is U-shaped and glacial, stretching back twenty-two miles into the Affric Mountains. As the ice thawed ten thousand years ago the meltwater streams created the broad, meandering flow of the river, which, on hitting a fault line in a wall of friable and ice-shattered conglomerate rock, washed out two separate channels, presenting us with a fifty-acre island, Eilean Aigas, bounded on both sides by a deep gorge with rushing falls and creating an ideal site for someone to come along and build a dam for hydro power, which was precisely what happened in the 1950s.

The gorge and the impressive Druim Falls, studded with rapids roiling round huge mid-stream rocks known as the Frogs, became a celebrated Victorian beauty spot and remains so, but the flooding of the falls by the hydro scheme caused the rapids to vanish, unless the river is very low when they re-emerge as foaming turbulence never quite breaking the surface. In a boat or canoe the going between damp and ferny seventy-foot walls is calm and eerily silent, but as you approach the flooded falls the flow suddenly springs into life as it grounds upon the submerged rocks, heaping up over them, carrying the air with them so that you are engulfed in rushing and streaming chevrons of white water.

The hydro dam (20-megawatt generation) undoubtedly cramped the gorge's tourist appeal, but not for the birds.

The high, vertical cliffs stretching for a quarter of a mile are ideal as a secure nest site and are variously occupied by jackdaws, kestrels and peregrines, grey wagtails and dippers as well as the ravens, while cormorants whitewash the rocks with guano as they haul out on the Frogs to hang their oil-less feathers out to dry.

★     ★     ★

Time was – and not so very long ago – the carrion-eating raven was aggressively persecuted right across Britain. With the historical exception of those at the Tower of London, the bird was despised by farmers, gamekeepers, landowners and shooting interests. Its very blackness was the signal for vilification and, wherever possible, annihilation. Little wonder they retreated to the far-flung mountain wilds and inaccessible coastal cliffs of the UK – this in marked contrast to Ireland where, in a gentler agricultural and less rapacious game-shooting culture, ravens were seen as useful scavengers and cleaners-up of the countryside, much helped by their legendary and fabled status in Celtic folklore and mythology. As a consequence Irish ravens live alongside human activities, frequenting farms, woods and country towns just as other crows do. Every ruined castle in rural Ireland usually has at least one pair of ravens nesting in it.

In Iceland ravens are common and fearless. They raid the racks of drying cod and mix with gulls as the fishing boats unload their catches, and it is from the old Norse *hrafn* that they arrive at their name. In far-flung Svalbard there is no real conflict with humans and no one thinks twice about a raven. They hang about the only town of Longyearbyen, scavenging from rubbish dumps. If a dead whale or a walrus is washed ashore they flock in to squabble over it like hyenas. The Inuit and other northern native peoples revered the raven, deeply embedded in their mythology and folklore, according it god-like status, and wore carved ivory and bone shamanic fetishes of the birds to ensure good hunting. The Inuit believed that the raven created the world.

Here in the Highlands things are very different. When I came to live here in the late sixties, if you were lucky enough to see a raven at all it was either dead or always a fleeing silhouette quickly vanishing over a lonely mountain horizon. Even offshore in the Outer Hebrides and the Small Isles ravens were extremely wary of the sight of man and it is probably only the acute intelligence of the species that enabled its survival at all.

Back in those days I knew a deer-stalker employed by a local sporting estate who always, as a matter of course, left the gralloch (Gaelic for intestines) of the shot deer on the mountainside laced with strychnine from a little aspirin bottle he kept in his waistcoat pocket: 'For eagles, hoodies and ravens,' he would growl, with a Machiavellian gleam in his eye. He is long dead and some of the traditions and values of his generation have progressed to a more tolerant culture, although such illegal practices still cast a shameful shadow over the nature-conservation successes of recent decades.

Not any more in this neck of the Highland woods, I am

pleased to relate. The advent of wildlife tourism as an economic force, legal protection and a wider conservation understanding has permitted raven numbers to increase and the birds to nest at least in some areas, unmolested. They are now part of our daily lives. I listen out for the guttural 'cronk, cronk' as they pass overhead every day. If a solitary black bird rows into view (rooks are almost never solitary), I stop what I'm doing to look for the wedge-shaped tail or to get the measure of its bulk to distinguish it from carrion or hooded crows. As the years have flicked by, their daily appearance here, their criss-crossing of the glen from high moor to hill, has become predictable, a reassuring norm, something we note with pleasure, and a characterful addition to our resident avifauna.

Confident of that interest, as a chunky silhouette crosses or that unmistakable plunking call reverberates from the woods, I don't hesitate to point and call to my friends and field centre colleagues, 'Ha! Raven!', yet I find myself still wary of my audience. Those farmers and crofters aplenty who charge ravens with killing lambs and many, not just old-school, gamekeepers are quick to condemn all crows, but especially hoodies and ravens, and will still do their utmost to kill them. 'The croaking raven doth bellow for revenge.' (*Hamlet*, Act III, scene ii.)

This autumn, when two rutting stags engaged in a head-to-head tussle, they were unfortunate in choosing an old fence line high on the moors as their duelling ground. One beast became entangled in rusty old wire and, when vanquished, was unable to escape. Whether he died from the vengeful lunges of the other stag, or whether he starved, we never discovered, but his carcass was quickly found and stripped to bare bones by the ravens. I heard them calling to each other across the hills, talking in that funereal, monosyllabic bassoon chatter, gathering numbers from afar as if by doing so their chances of being ambushed would be greatly reduced or, perhaps more likely, cementing their cryptic social structure by sharing the spoils of such rich pickings. Like vultures on the Serengeti, ravens seemed to appear from nowhere. It was the presence of more than twenty flighting in that told us the carcass was there. As I approached they rose up in cronking alarm while I was still hundreds of yards away, the morning air momentarily blackened by their panicky departure.

On occasions I have staked out a carcass to enjoy watching ravens or to show them to others. I built a tree-top hide looking out over the moor for just that purpose, but I quickly discovered that, even though the birds have enjoyed a comeback, their long history of persecution has left its mark. They are extremely wary of people or of anything suspicious. Raven intelligence is legendary and has been comprehensively researched by scientists and naturalists throughout the raven range.

My wildlife cameraman friend Lindsay McCrae, who works with the BBC Natural History Unit, tells me with much frustration but a lot of admiration that when filming ravens from a hide he discovered that at a hundred yards they could tell the difference between a real telephoto lens sticking out of a camouflaged hide and a mock one left in place when Lindsay wasn't there. In our own tree-top bird hide, an observer sneezing or absentmindedly pulling out a handkerchief to blow his nose would be spotted at two hundred and fifty yards' range and would cause the ravens to disappear for several hours at a stretch. In Scotland it is still very difficult to get close to a wild raven.

*       *       *

Many years ago I was heading for home from a lengthy hill walk in our local mountains. It was early March and I had grown weary of the winter and of being stuck indoors. I took to the hills knowing very well that the days were still short, that the snows were by no means past and that mountain weather could be as treacherous as any ocean squall. Foolish is he who goes to the mountains unprepared. The day dawned bright and cloudless. I was able to push uphill quickly in strong sunshine, a welcome surge of early spring warmth at my back. But as it wore on a sinister cloud bank began to muster in the west. Ignoring the signals I hurried on, keen to traverse a high ridge where the wind had scoured away the snows leaving the smooth, lichenous tundra as easy walking.

In startling white winter plumage, ptarmigan rose from under my feet, scuttling away among the rocks or belching like drunks as they flew over the cornice and disappeared from view in a pied flurry of sunlit wings and coal-black outer tail feathers. Suddenly the sun was gone and a scowling wall of snow cloud breached the ridge on a scything wind that swirled with the first flakes of what would become, with terrifying speed, a white-out blizzard. I knew I had to get off the ridge, but in the direction I needed to go the rock fell away beneath a near-vertical snow cornice built up over months of winter and frost – always an extremely dangerous winter feature – falling to a precipitous boulder field that cascaded a thousand feet to a steep snow slope far below.

Just before the blizzard engulfed me I found a place where the cornice had collapsed and the reliable rock underneath stood out, grey and solid. It was a relief to escape from that wind. Very gingerly I scrambled down into the boulder field, easing myself between rocks as big as bungalows. I needed to get down, down to a lower and safer altitude before the storm closed off my retreat. I ran, scrambled and slithered, leaping from snow drift to glissading slope, steeply down as fast as I dared. I must have descended at least six or seven hundred feet in a few minutes and was happy for it. But not for long. The blizzard came roaring in behind me so thick and fast that in seconds I could see nothing. I could barely see my own boots, let alone where I was placing my feet. I knew I couldn't go on.

I groped my way to a huge boulder and crawled in under its lee. I cut a small snow cave with my hands and, thinking it would pass, lay down to wait it out. For perhaps half an hour I was safe enough. It was still only three o'clock and I had plenty of daylight left. But the storm was just getting going. The wind shrieking over the mountain crest was creating a vortex below, into which the snow was being sucked. It fell thicker and heavier and the wind swirled angrily round me. Snow heaped in, smothering my boulder in just a few minutes with a thick blanket, which, scoured by the wind, broke and fell across my shallow cave so that it began to fill. I realised I had to move or be buried alive.

I crawled out into that blizzard not knowing where I was going, except down, painfully slowly, groping forward like a blind man, testing each step for firmness, hugging the rocks, stumbling often. There seemed to be no let-up. The storm raged above me in the high tops with the roar of a train emerging from a tunnel. At best, visibility was three feet. For an hour I crept insect-like down that mountain slope. I had only the vaguest idea where I was until, quite suddenly, the wind dropped, the snow withdrew to a few floating flakes and, for a handful of fleeting minutes, I glimpsed the palest of suns veiled in a woollen shroud.

Only twenty feet away, right in front of me, was a preci-pice. Had I blundered on, gone unwittingly to its edge, one step could have plummeted me a hundred feet to the rocks below. I remember my heart bursting inside my chest. That enfeebled sun had come to my rescue. It gave me just long enough to see my way round the precipice to a further boulder field and scree slope where I could safely continue downwards. But yet again the sun fled and the snow came rampaging back in huge, sticky flakes thicker than ever. Heart still thumping from the fright, I knew I had to sit it out again; far too dangerous to blunder on. I found another big boulder and crawled round it on all fours to find the most sheltered nook. I was not alone.

As I settled in, my eyes focused on something very black about five feet away. I stared at it through the blizzard. Slowly I made out a twiggy mound jammed between the rocks. Hunkered down within its bowl was a raven. A raven! I had wanted to see a wild raven close up for years. There it was on the nest, only five feet away. I could almost touch it. I had never been so close to a living wild raven. I froze – not that I had much choice. I was safe for now, and relatively comfortable, enjoying what scant shelter the rock afforded me. So I sat and watched the snow land on the raven's back and slowly turn it to marble.

A little while later the storm drifted away again and the snow withdrew to a few feathery flakes. The raven raised her head and fixed me suspiciously with eyes like black pearls. Her great bill turned towards me and her long primaries shuffled nervously. Had she recognised me as even half human? It seemed that behind the gleaming eye her astute raven brain was weighing the odds. To fly, exposing her chicks to the snow, or to sit it out and see what this intruder proved to be? I can hardly have looked very human and I certainly wasn't behaving in a predatory way. I was in a place where she had never seen a human before; she was closer to a man than she ever had been, without knowing or under-standing how I had got there. I was lying down; I was silent and motionless and, like her, I was snow-dappled from woolly hat to gaitered boots – a most unconvincing killer of ravens. Very slowly her head lowered once more until her great black bill was resting on the rim of the nest. Her eye closed, the pale lower lid lifting uncertainly until the pearl was gone.

I can't remember now how long I lay there. Several more times the snow barged in and out again, flailing around me like an unruly child. In the clear breaks the raven would awaken, look round, then sink back again. Every few minutes she would wake up with a start, as if she had heard something, look round and subside once more, back to fulfilling the tedious obligation of all chick-minding mothers.

I was fascinated but I knew I had to go. I needed to get down the mountain before dark and I still had several miles to walk to reach my car. Just as I was about to move, through the snow haze came a sharp flurry of black wings. It was her mate. He pitched on the rock beside her and emitted a loud, deep 'cronk', a sound ragged with dark authority, like a blast from a klaxon.

The hen raven rose up and shook the snow from her wings and tail, stepping back to the nest edge, even closer to me so that I could see her every feather. She stood proud and handsome. Beneath her massive bill her throat was a shaggy boa of black feathers. Her legs were scaled like snake skin, each long toe tipped with a hooked black claw. Her tail was long and bluntly pointed, like a trench shovel. She answered her mate with a staccato series of clicks and 'urk' sounds in a muted conversation barely audible above the swirling wind.

As the male stepped forward, so the chicks – I was never sure how many, probably four – thrust their ugly, bulging, blind-eyed heads into the air and gaped their vulgar yellow-rimmed throats, red and huge, like so many lurid cactus blooms wobbling on extended stalks. The male bird belched noisily and regurgitated a foul, multi-coloured ragout of putrid carrion, thrusting it into the yawning gapes with indelicate precision.

I had to descend before the snowstorm visited further life-threatening horrors upon me in the dimming light of late afternoon. I was no novice in the mountains and I knew very well how dangerous they can be if one is caught out and forced to spend a night among them. I stood up. Both adult birds stared at me in a fleeting moment of utter disbelief before they leaped together into the bitter wind, clashing pinions in their panic to go.

# 9

# A Dog's Life

January, it seemed, had done its worst. As the month free-
wheeled to a close, that same un-winterish breeze from the
south had swung slowly to the south-west, staying there,
prevailing, soft, damp and beguilingly felicitous. The
Highlands' craggy face was splashed with light rain, fresh-
ening the winter grass and the whiskery lichens that adorn
our trees, like green-grey tinsel. The snow had vanished
from the hills. Surely winter couldn't be over yet. It had
fooled me, not just the great tits, for a week, drawing life
out of winter crannies so that suddenly there was birdsong
and bustle everywhere I looked.

The badgers knew it. They emerged and tore up frost-
killed grass and bracken with their teeth and claws, rolling
it together and shuffling backwards with it tucked under
their chins, down into the dark ventricles of their setts
for fresh bedding. At one entrance I placed a slice of dry
hay bale from the stables just to see if they would take
it. It vanished that night, scarcely a stem left, whisked

underground without a second thought. After some essential housekeeping, they foraged for earthworms across the lawns and the moles joined them, heaving their tumps of spoil into a chain of mini-volcanoes of crumbly brown loam.

Every afternoon I walked, quietly watching and wondering what effect these sudden moods of unseasonable weather were having on our wildlife. Did it matter that the great tits got fired up a month too early? Would they adjust their nesting calendar? Would the essential caterpillars they need to feed their chicks on be available at the right moment if they started nesting now? And what if the frost and snow returned? If all the looping caterpillars the great tits habitually rear their chicks on were killed off too? Could they cope? And if they lost that brood of chicks to starvation and the cold, would the parent birds just start again later on? Would the earthworms be able to retreat?

The badgers would be all right, I was sure. They would duck below ground and curl up again, refreshed and strengthened by the nourishment they had taken in. Similarly the pipistrelle bats. They don't mind coming out of hibernation at all. They can dip in and out of their torpor several times in a winter without penalty. But what of the moths I see the bats snatching at night from around the outside lights? Can they close down again? Go back to their crevices and chill, literally, or are they caught out by the next cold snap, immobilised and rigid, so that their energy resources are burned up prematurely? Do entire generations of moths perish, or just a few, or perhaps none at all?

It is the invertebrates that trouble me. They are the uncountable legions from which whole food chains build, eking energy directly or indirectly from the great universal gift of carbohydrate that surrounds us and passing it on to a myriad higher organisms. Without the bugs the swallows can't skim the summer skies; the brown trout, the otter and the osprey would fade away; the rooks would fail and the goshawk would vanish for ever into the dark woods.

But hasn't this happened many times before in the millions of years our wildlife has been evolving? Ice ages have waxed and waned. This glen was covered with an ice sheet three thousand feet thick as recently as twelve thousand years ago, a mere blink of an evolutionary eye. Surely their long genes conceal a trump card to get them through. What aces we have never dreamed of are encrypted into the dizzy spirals of their DNA?

While all these thoughts fizzed around my brain I found myself walking aimlessly towards the top of the garden through a spring-like chorus of birdsong brought on by a sudden salvo of low sun. Robins, wrens, great and blue tits, dunnocks, and a blackbird alarming at my presence led me to a corner of neglected shrubbery ruled by rampant rhododendrons and labyrinthine laurels, a ragged yew clump and some towering *thujas* – western red cedars from north-west America – planted 130 years ago during the Victorian craze for exotic conifers.

It was in the ancient hollow stump of one of these trees that I once found a hedgehog hibernating, curled like a fist and swaddled in moss and leaves. Checking it out was easy this time. The stump was empty, as I'd known it would be. Our hedgehogs have disappeared in recent years. It is rare to see one now, even on the roads. I am suspicious that the on-off winters of recent years have tricked them. In a run of days as mild as this they could so easily come out of hibernation, find nothing to eat and then be unable to go back. They starve.

And I had another reason for visiting this tucked-away grotto of the unkempt garden. It is where sparrowhawks often come to pluck their prey. Many times I have found the tell-tale scatter of feathers beneath the gnarled old yews. Sparrowhawks will kill and pluck their prey almost anywhere if they are not disturbed.

During the spring and summer months when the hawks can hunt in good daylight at four in the morning, it's not unusual to find the signs on the lawns right out in the open. But when there are people or dogs about they will cart their prey off gripped in their needle talons, often still alive, to some familiar shady corner where they can feed unseen and undisturbed, often using a stump as an altar for their dire executions. As Alfred, Lord Tennyson had it:

> A sparhawk proud did hold in wicked jail
> Music's sweet chorister, the Nightingale
> To whom with sighs she said: 'O set me free,
> And in my song I'll praise no bird but thee.'
> The Hawk replied: 'I will not lose my diet
> To let a thousand such enjoy their quiet.'

There is no doubt that sparrowhawks stake out our bird feeders and tables. It is a common complaint from suburban gardeners who love and feed their birds. Both species of British true hawks (those with rounded wings – *accipiters*, not *falcons*), the goshawk and the sparrowhawk, are masters of guerrilla warfare; ambush is their primary tactic, the art of surprise followed by a sudden snatch raid of dazzling speed. Of course it distresses people to see their favourite robin or chaffinch snatched right in front of their windows, and it happens to us. I have often pondered the many ways in which we advantage or disadvantage our wildlife by interfering with natural selection. There are no easy answers, but on balance, although bird feeders and tables probably provide an easier hunt for sparrowhawks, feeding the birds enables them to survive hard winters and consequently to breed more successfully. I erect chicken-wire foils around our tables with the mesh sizes large enough for sparrows, chaffinches and tits to slip through, but which frustrate the hawks' first surprise attack. They work well.

When a snatch is successful the hawk doesn't kill the prey instantly, like a falcon's stoop usually does: it has to fly to an undisturbed site with the wretched chaffinch – chaffinches are very commonly taken – in its talons and only then does it kill it. The ghastly plucking begins. The curved beak, as sharp as a fishhook, clears back the feathers and goes for the jugular. The helpless prey is plucked alive until its arteries are ripped asunder and the blood pulses out. The bigger the bird, the longer and messier the kill. Nature observes no cruelty; killing is its daily round.

As J. A. Baker famously wrote in his classic work, *The Peregrine*:

> The word 'predator' is baggy with misuse. All birds eat living flesh at some time in their lives. Consider the cold-eyed thrush, that springy carnivore of lawns, worm stabber, basher to death of snails. We should not sentimentalise his song and forget the killing that sustains it.

My instincts were sound. Sure enough, there had been a recent kill and the altar had not been a tree stump but a boulder marking the grave of a dog. I bent to examine the feathers – black-barred, brown and cinnamon through to bright henna: a woodcock. I was surprised. Woodcock aren't on the sparrowhawk's regular menu. I suspect they are too well camouflaged, blending almost miraculously into their woodland habitat. But these were not normal times.

Many of our winter woodcock are Scandinavian and Russian migrants, arriving in December in thousands and dispersing quickly into woodland habitats far and wide. Unlike other waders, particularly the shorebirds such as curlew, knot, redshank or dunlin, woodcock are not gregarious. They live lonely, undercover lives of secrecy and covert undertakings. We rarely see them unless they are flushed out of dense thickets by the dogs, when their characteristic graceful, looping flight wings them silently away through the trees. This one was caught out – not by frost, but perhaps it, too, was fazed by the sudden, unseasonal upward lurch of the thermometer. Perhaps it had ventured too far out of its mossy and ferny thickets. The burning dandelion eye of the sparrowhawk misses very little.

★    ★    ★

In the dense shade of the old yew clump there is not just one dog grave, but a line of similar stones. Six, to be exact. Five rough boulders in a row and one a cut stone with an inscription: 'Max, 1968–1981' and something in Latin underneath. I dropped the woodcock feathers and bent to rub the moss off the stone. I had certainly not forgotten the dog, but I had momentarily forgotten the inscription. I love to come here quietly to remember them all and the decades they span: the Labradors, Max and Jubilee; Hobson, my first Jack Russell; Butch, another Labrador; then Rough and Tumble, two more Jack Russell brothers. The most recent is little Tumble, whose valiant terrier heart finally failed after fifteen years of constant, unwavering loyalty.

We didn't plan it, but dogs have always been an important ingredient in our Highland lives. My first, Max, a yellow Labrador, was bright, alert, desperate to please and, as a consequence, very easy to train. I learned early that a well-trained dog was a useful adjunct to studying wildlife. Over the thirteen years of his life, Max found hundreds of ground-nesting birds without ever harming one. He would tell me with a glance and a wag of the tail if we were close to deer or foxes, hares or rabbits; he located exciting finds, such as capercaillie, ptarmigan, dotterel and woodcock nests, wildcat dens, otter holts, new-born roe deer fawns and, on one occasion, a woman who had suffered a heart attack and collapsed into deep heather in the dark. Max saved her life; we rushed her to the hospital just in time. On many more occasions, by adopting the 'set' position and freezing at a scent, he would warn me that other wildlife had recently passed through.

If you've had an exceptional dog, when it dies and you want to replace it, the spectre of invidious comparisons looms up, like a fog. Max was my bachelor dog. He was my only child and loved one, my constant companion through good times and bad, the more cherished because I had nursed him back from puppy distemper at nine weeks old, and because he bridged two great changes in my life: the first, moving from England to forge a home and a career in the Highlands, and the second, marriage and the birth of my children.

Only ten days after collecting him from the breeder Max had become wretched and fevered; a blond, limp bundle unable even to lift his head. The vets told me there was no hope. Reluctant to give in, and more out of distraction than from expectation, I teased drops of milk and glucose into his throat through a pipette. He clung on. By day he lived inside my shirt and at night I fell asleep with my hand on him in my bed in an attempt to monitor his fluttering heartbeat. After a week he began to rally, and after three weeks, I knew he would pull through. I had a puppy again, but by some unforeseen mutual alchemy a special bond had taken root.

He grew up to be intelligent, intuitive and loyal beyond any definition of absolute dedication I could have imagined.

He became my shadow, redefining the expression 'dogging my heels', travelling everywhere with me in my car. Pleasing me seemed to be his entire life's purpose.

Training him was a mutual-adoration process: I was keen to fulfil his soaring ambition to please and he was desperate to succeed. It was as though I could teach him almost anything I wished and he would grasp it as soon as we had begun. I hung tassels onto lever door handles and he quickly learned to pull them open, then push them closed behind him, letting himself in and out of my cottage. He had an excellent nose and could search and retrieve over great distances. His mouth was as soft as jelly; I trained him on hen's eggs and never once did he break or drop one, delivering them delicately into my hand as if each was a precious gift.

Once, when he was about six years old, I took a group of field centre visitors to the summit of a four thousand-foot mountain in Glen Affric on a fine June day to search for the exquisitely delicate, red- and pink-flowered alpine azalea, *Loiseleuria procumbens*, which creeps an inch high over the thin tundra summit. It was a long walk in – over four miles – and another mile of steep, breathless haul to the ridge. We found and photographed our azalea and ate our sandwiches at the summit cairn in brilliant sunshine. Max settled down beside me and fell asleep. Then we slowly headed down. At the bottom of the mountain a woman named Kirsty suddenly realised she had left her binoculars at the cairn. She wanted to go back, but I pointed out it would take at least an hour and a half. It was already four in the afternoon with more than four miles still to walk to our vehicle and five other guests all keen to get home for tea. I could not let her go back up the mountain on her own.

I told her not to worry and that I would return for them myself the following day. She wasn't happy with that, worried that it would rain or the binoculars might be stolen by other climbers. It was a tricky moment. I could feel the others glaring at me, all agitating to get home. I looked at Max. A proposition loomed up that might allow us all to continue walking out. 'It's just possible,' I ventured, not really believing it was, 'that Max will go back and get them for you.' There were incredulous looks all round, but over several days they had seen how roundly trained he was and not even Kirsty chose to challenge me.

I took her cardigan and held it to his nose. I rubbed his ears affectionately, pointed back up the trail and called, 'High lost!' He set off back up the path at a fast lope. The last we saw of him was his thick otter tail gyrating enthusiastically as he vanished into the grassy contours of the mountain. We started the long walk out.

An hour later the sun had gone and we arrived at our vehicle cold and tired. I kept looking over my shoulder – no sign of Max. Everyone loaded their rucksacks into the Land Rover, some changed their boots, others stood about looking apprehensive. An uneasy silence had descended over us all. It had been a long, arduous day and my guests were getting stiff. No Max. 'Jump in,' I urged, as nonchalantly as I could. 'I'm not worried about Max. I'll run you home and come straight back for him.'

It was the last thing I wanted to do, an extra thirty-six

miles there and back, but I couldn't really keep them waiting any longer. I fired up the engine and turned the vehicle round. Just as I was about to let the clutch up there was an electrifying gasp from everyone on board, then a cheer as they all tumbled out of the vehicle. Down the track, still fifty yards away, Max was padding towards us with a pair of black binoculars held firmly in his mouth. His tail was wagging energetically; his eyes shone with unfettered canine pride. Kirsty burst into tears.

I hated to be parted from Max even for a day. On the occasions that I had to go away we both pined and I came home to rapturous, whole body-wagging welcomes to the very end of his long life. At the age of thirteen – a good age for a Labrador – he suffered a stroke and a little while later he died, swiftly and painlessly, with his head in my lap. I mourned him then and I mourn him now. I knew in my bones I would never have another dog like Max. Such is the price of love that, whether we resist it or not, some small part of us dies with the beloved so that, as we emerge from the moment, we know in our hearts that nothing can ever be quite the same again.

I buried Max beside the yew grove and planted thirteen daffodil bulbs on his grave, one for every year of his blessed life. Soon afterwards, honouring a local Highland tradition – many country houses have dog cemeteries with walls or railings around them – I erected a small stone carved with a Latin inscription, *Quo non praestantior alter*, written of loyal Misenus, son of Aeolus, of whom in Virgil's 'Æneid' it is said, 'Than whom none more excellent'.

I missed him terribly. Life seemed wearisome without a dog, the days empty, the house and the car strangely unwelcoming. But I knew I did not want another Labrador. The notion that I could just go out and buy a replacement seemed unthinkable, an alien country I had no stomach to visit. The very idea seemed a betrayal to Max and an injustice to any new dog, which, through no fault of its own, was never likely to be able to meet my galactic expectations. Besides, a son of Max from a local friend's Labrador bitch, a lovely gentle dog called Jubilee (born in 1976), had been given to my small children. He was a perfect children's dog, gentle, adoring, adored and adorable, but he was theirs, not mine, and nothing I could do would ever change that. So I scoured the livestock column of the local paper until I found something completely different. A Jack Russell terrier puppy for ten pounds. When I arrived at the house in the back streets of Inverness to a barrage of frantic barking from a bobbery pack of adult terriers of deeply dubious lineage, I thought I had made a mistake.

There wasn't much choice – only one left. So I called him Hobson and took him home, not at all sure what I'd bought. Nicknamed Hobdog by my children, he matured to be a splendid little character: loyal, feisty, tireless, endlessly enthusiastic and a wonderful companion. He went everywhere with me. He was as much my dog as Max had been, but he was also entirely different: the self-willed nature of the terrier breed made him an indomitable character and much more testing to train. But I loved him for it.

Long before his time Hobson became ill with an

inoperable bowel tumour. Faced with unacceptable suffering, I pulled the plug. I gritted my teeth and wept tears of betrayal as I buried him with more daffodils beside Max in this quiet place at the top of the garden.

Once again I went searching for another dog. Lucy was enthusiastic about another Jack Russell, so we put the word about among our friends. We hit lucky. There was a litter only a few miles away. We went to look and immediately fell for a fat little fellow, then only four weeks old, one of six smooth-haired pups in a huge cardboard box, all white with expressive black and tan faces and random black blobs dotted about their bodies as if someone had spilt ink on them. We would return at nine weeks.

It is fifteen years ago now that I went with Lucy and my youngest daughter Hermione, then at the puppy-obsessed age of just six, to collect the one we had ordered, later named Rough. Only two remained in the box, all the others had gone, mostly as working dogs to gamekeepers. The breeder lifted Rough out and handed him to the girls. I found myself staring down at the tiny, stunted remnant, half the size of his brother, shivering in the pathos of abandonment at the bottom of the box. 'What will happen to that?' I asked naïvely, not even knowing its sex.

'No one's going to want him,' came the stark retort. 'He's a runt. He should have been drowned at birth.' So, to our small daughter's uncontainable delight, Rough and Tumble came home together.

Perpetually bowled over and shoved aside by his clumsy, rumbustious brother, who was almost twice his weight, from the very beginning Tumble attracted pity. We fell for it willingly and spoiled him rotten. He loved it and learned quickly to exploit it. A runt he might have been, but there was nothing wrong with his brain – he was far brighter than his brother. He never grew to match Rough's weight, strength or speed so what he lacked in brawn he had to achieve by guile. When there was food in the offing he could shovel on the charm and roll out the special pleading by the barrowful. It always worked. He came out on top. OK, he wasn't very robust, his coat was thin and he felt the cold, he couldn't breathe silently through his nose and he lacked the gutsy, feisty, randy characteristics of Rough and most other Jack Russells, but he possessed other, far subtler skills.

He could spot a soft touch a mile away and knew how to curl up in your lap and make you feel the most important person on the planet. We all adored Tumble. But at eight years old the defective genes that had branded him a runt finally returned to haunt him. An unseen internal physical defect caught up with him and plonked him firmly in the last-chance saloon.

Let me be clear: I am not sentimental about my animals. I love them as much or more than anyone else, and can be as soppy as the next man, but I will not stand by and watch them suffer. I have shot my dogs and my horses when there was no way out of their pain; blown out their brains in a final act of respect and oblation – a personal covenant I cannot and would not delegate to another. So when one day I noticed Tumble straining unnaturally to defecate, my heart sank. I thought I knew where we were headed. I had lost

Hobson to a horrid bowel problem and I didn't like the look of this at all. We tried laxatives to no avail. Volcano-like and ominous, a bulge appeared around his tail. To begin with it was soft and painless – not like a tumour – so I guessed it was a rectal hernia.

Town or country, when your dog is ill, it's a crisis, in our case made worse by living up a remote Highland glen. John Easton, our friendly local vet, is only twelve miles away and regularly comes to attend to our horses and cattle. He confirmed my suspicions: thankfully not a tumour, but two hernias not just a single, one on either side of his tail. 'Sorry,' John shook his head, 'there's nothing I can do. There's no medical treatment or cure. Your only hope is a risky and complicated operation with no guarantee of success.' Worse still, John couldn't attempt the surgery himself, it would have to be Glasgow: the highly respected University of Glasgow Veterinary Hospital, on busy summer roads a drive of four gruelling hours.

Tumble had become my dog. Once again I had a shadow, always there, always pleased to see me, always keen to join in with whatever I was doing. And in the evenings he would curl up on my lap in my fireside chair, snoring and dreaming in that oceanic slumber of contentment only a dog can know.

All summer the condition worsened. We kept him going on liquid paraffin. In front we had an alert, happy, healthy, fun-loving terrier; behind he was pained, distorted, grotesque, eventually unable even to wag his little tail. When I took him out it was taking him up to half an hour to evacuate pathetic caterpillars of excrement, and then only with my help containing the obscene bulges on either side of his tail with my hands. Daily they grew larger. Incontinence followed, the internal pressure overcoming him so suddenly that he wallowed helplessly in the pathos of his own distress.

'Do we risk the surgery?' I asked Lucy and Hermione, now eleven, who had hijacked both puppies five years before and, although she had reluctantly conceded Tumble to me and made Rough her special dog, her own constant companion, she had always doted on them both.

'Daddy,' she said to me, fighting back tears and in a voice I had not heard before, 'you are to try *everything*.' I phoned for an appointment in Glasgow.

A few days later we were there, Tumble and I, face to face with a smiling young Australian surgeon named Ross. I stood Tumble carefully on the stainless-steel examination bench. Ross was pulling on surgical gloves. 'I need to investigate the extent of the hernias. Will you hold him firm?'

'Sure,' I said, and to Tumble, 'Sorry, little man, he's going to stick a finger up your bum.' It hurt and he yelled, and I felt a traitor for having to hold him so tight. 'Sorry,' I murmured again, when it was over, burying my face in his velvet ears. 'Please don't stop trusting me just yet. Can you fix it, Ross?' I asked.

He promised he would do his best but warned that if it failed there would be only one outcome. There was a moment of silence, broken only by the slap of the rubber gloves springing off his fingers. Hermione's words swirled round my brain. 'Do we give it a go?' he asked at length.

I liked his honest eyes, and his bare, scrubbed forearms

seemed to evince an inner strength. This young man had the air of a real professional. Sometimes I think Aussies are more straightforward than us Brits; I trusted this one instinctively. I nodded. Just for a moment I had no words.

I had to leave him, of course, and trail back up north through the wide, empty mountains to our lonely Inverness-shire glen, the lonelier for Tumble's absence and made more poignant by Hermione's tears and Rough's whining restlessness. Three days passed, then the phone call.

Ross said it was much worse than he had expected. When he opened Tumble up he'd found the whole bowel distorted and doubled back on itself in an S-shape. He'd had to straighten it by hitching it permanently to the abdomen wall. Then he darned the splits in the ruptured muscles where the hernias bulged, stitching them together in a mesh of zigzagged sutures. The little dog had come round, but he was sedated and drowsy. They wanted to hold on to him until the bowel moved, to see if it was going to work – the crucial test. It would be another day or two perhaps.

The next day a friendly Glaswegian nurse phoned: Tumble had eaten a little, but still no movement. Another twenty-four hours dragged by. It was the same the following morning – still nothing. It might be better, she suggested, if I came down and took him home . . . 'Some dogs are very particular about where they go.' That's my Tumble, I thought, and ran for the car.

In three and a half hours I was there, pacing the corridor, like a prisoner awaiting sentence. The door opened. I knelt to greet him. The same small, blotched black and white face with tan eyebrows, the little black nose, the same eyes of polished oak, ears cocked in woozy recognition, only a bald patch on his neck where the anaesthetic had been. For a moment I held his head in my hands, staring into those deep, unreproving eyes. Could he possibly understand why I had abandoned him?

It was just as well I was braced for his rear end to be a mess. His underbelly, tail and backside were shaved to the pink, the whole region angry and swollen, sutured like a Christmas turkey right down his belly and round his unhappy tail. Gingerly I carried him out to the car. 'We need a good movement to know if the bowel is working properly,' smiled another kind assistant as I left. 'Please give us a ring and let us know.'

On the way home I stopped to stretch my legs on the one thousand five hundred and eight-foot high-point of the Drumochter, the high mountain pass that separates mellow Tayside from rugged old Inverness-shire where the treeless hills veer skywards to the clouds on both sides of the road. Tumble looked up from the blankets as if he wanted to do the same. 'OK,' I said, 'gently does it.'

He wobbled out onto the deer-cropped sward, looking round at the fragrant, cooling hills of late summer, as if to say, 'This is more like it.' He stood still for several minutes, occasionally lifting his nose to test the air. Then he glanced up at me for reassurance before sniffing a tussock of rushes. He eased forward, went to cock his leg, winced with pain and thought better of it – after all, he had been gutted like a fish. He looked back to me for guidance.

'What a good boy,' I said reassuringly, in the voice I have always used when my dogs perform their functions satisfactorily. I wanted him to have another go, however sore he was. I know how vital kidneys are. But something bigger was on his mind; he had grander designs than that. For a moment he looked nonplussed, eyeing first the mountains and then me before moving stiffly and purposefully to a place of his own particular choosing, an intimate amphitheatre of lawn encircled by a lilac pastel haze of fading heather. Awkwardly and painfully he bent to a faecal crouch. I held my breath. A moment later the finest, glossiest, roundest, most spectacular four-and-a-half-inch polony of healthy terrier excrement launched itself triumphantly into upland Perthshire. I never dreamed that I would be so thrilled to see a dog turd. Smiling broadly, I reached for my mobile phone.

# 10

# The Memory of Owls

The screech-owl, with ill-boding cry,
Portends strange things, old women say;
Stops every fool that passes by,
And frights the school-boy from his play.
   'The Politicians', Lady Mary Wortley Montagu


Then nightly sings the staring owl,
Tu-whoo!
Tu-whit! Tu-whoo! A merry note,
While greasy Joan doth keel the pot.
                    *Love's Labour's Lost,* Act V, scene ii,
                              William Shakespeare


I cannot be trusted with owls. I shot one once, with an air
rifle when I was a tearaway eleven-year-old, and the guilt
lives with me yet. A tawny habitually roosted in a thick,
incalculably ancient yew tree in the rambling garden of my
home. Tawny owls had probably been roosting there for
hundreds of years. The tree was not particularly tall – pruned
back many times over many centuries – but its trunk
possessed all the girth of great age, and from about fifteen
feet up its massed limbs erupted in a dense, unruly

candelabrum of branches, casting their shade and their shed ginger needles in a broad circle over stone paving slabs heaved chaotically upwards, like tectonic plates, by centuries of roots.

My grandfather had shown me that owl with pride. Together we peered up into the thicket of branches. There, close to the main stem, sat a brown owl with its eyes shut. 'There was a tawny owl in this tree when my grandfather was a boy,' he told me. It was arithmetic I couldn't fathom. My grandfather, very tall, bald and with gold-rimmed, half-moon spectacles perched on his nose, then well into his eighties, seemed to me to be as old as Noah, so the notion of his grandfather must surely have pre-dated not just the Flood, but the entire Old Testament. An unthinkable number of years and a wholly incalculable number of owls. I was awestruck.

That year I was given an air rifle, a BSA Meteor .477, with open sights. It was the most exciting birthday gift I had ever received. In the short space of a birthday afternoon I became Davy Crockett, Kit Carson and the Lone Ranger all rolled into one ill-disciplined puberulous youth bursting to tangle with danger and adventure. I was also given a packet of targets and some lessons from my father about handling guns. He made me learn by heart a rhyme that hung on the gunroom wall. It was called, appropriately, 'A Father's Advice':

> Never, never let your gun
> Pointed be at anyone.
> That it may unloaded be,
> Matters not the least to me.

I can recite it now as then. It was a sportsman's code of conduct with hearty Victorian overtones.

> If 'twixt you and neighbouring gun
> Bird may fly or beast may run,
> Let this maxim ere be thine,
> 'Follow not across the line.'

It would be years before I discovered what a maxim was, but I recited it confidently and won the freedom I craved. It ran to seven verses, with a finger-wagging couplet of dire consequences at the very end:

> You may kill or you may miss,
> But at all times think of this:
> All the pheasants ever bred
> Won't repay for one man dead.

At the age of eleven it seemed to me to have the authority of God. But it did not say, 'Don't shoot owls.'

In truth, the reverse was often the case. My grandfather, born a Victorian of the old school, was a shooting man – no, more than that, he was an excellent and widely respected shot. It was what sporting gentry of his generation did; a social shibboleth for acceptability obsessively adhered to by all who sought to move in those circles. Almost all country estates had shoots and employed gamekeepers. I have family game books detailing the staggering numbers of game birds shot – pheasants, partridges, snipe, grouse, duck and woodcock – dating back to the early nineteenth century. Two volumes of my grandfather's, commenced in 1898 in slanting copperplate handwriting when he was twenty, and running on uninterrupted up until he enlisted for the First World War, then on between the wars, reveals that he was in high demand. He was invited to shoots throughout the land, and every summer he travelled with his loader and his chauffeur to Scotland for the 'Glorious Twelfth' of August and the opening of the grouse season, first to the Campsie Fells, thence to Inverness-shire and Morayshire and on up to Sutherland for September deer-stalking.

It remains undeniably the case that those nineteenth- and early-twentieth-century shooting estates, both great and small, operated a systematic annihilation of any wildlife that might presume to threaten a game bird, and many more that didn't. There were no meaningful wildlife protection laws until the middle of the twentieth century, no influential million-plus membership organisations, such as the RSPB and the Wildlife Trusts today. As a movement, nature conservation was a gleam in one or two visionary individuals' eyes. Ecology as a science and a profession hadn't been invented. Countryside and wildlife management was essentially the preserve of those private individuals who owned the land and everything that inhabited it.

Gamekeepers ruled their beats with snares, gin traps, poison baits and the gun – and with impunity. Anything with a hooked beak, including owls, was shot on sight. The animals and birds that fell prey to their grim labours became a currency. Gamekeepers were not just assessed by the spectacular 'bags' of game – mostly pheasants, partridges and grouse – they produced for their employers and guests, but by the total numbers of 'vermin' they destroyed in the process.

In order to demonstrate proof of their dire professionalism, in the woods gamekeepers erected macabre gibbets for their victims. As a boy I remember examining these with morbid fascination. Lengths of wooden fence rail nailed to a tree in a prominent position, for an employer to see and approve, would often display the withered and shrunken corpses of crows, jays, weasels, stoats, sparrowhawks, buzzards, kestrels, peregrines, hedgehogs and, yes, often owls, all hanging in a row like bedraggled coats on pegs. In his book *The Amateur Poacher* (1879), the eminent nineteenth-century naturalist and writer Richard Jefferies stumbles across a gamekeeper's gibbet on the outside wall of a 'ruinous' old wooden shed deep in the Wiltshire woods, 'proof', he writes, 'of the keeper's loyal activity':

> Along the back there were three rows of weasels and stoats nailed through the head and neck to the planks . . . a hundred in each row . . . about three hundred altogether. But the end of the shed was the place where the more distinguished offenders were gibbeted . . . four rows of crows, magpies and jays. Hawks filled the third row. The kestrels were the most numerous, but there were many sparrow-hawks . . . and the remains of a smaller bird . . . a merlin. But the last and lowest row . . . was the most striking.
>
> This grand tier was crowded with owls. Clearly this gallery was constantly renewed . . . the white [barn] owl side by side

> with brown wood [tawny] owls . . . and a few long horned
> [long-eared] owls. Trap and gun have so reduced the wood
> owls that you may listen half the night and never hear the
> 'whoo-hoo' that seems to demand your name.

What Jefferies makes entirely clear is that this was the norm. Nowhere in this comprehensive description does he express any surprise or shock at his find. It was quite simply what happened on all shoots, a major modification of the natural world that would persist well into the twentieth century.

The naturalist James Edmund Harting wrote in his 1872 *The Ornithology of Shakespeare*: 'Alas . . . that we should live to see our noble falcons gibbeted, like thieves, upon the "keeper's tree".' In some remote corners of Britain these illegal and unenlightened practices and traditions still persist. Disturbingly, a gamekeeper on a grouse moor in Scotland was prosecuted for shooting a short-eared owl as recently as 2004.

I was reared in the dying decades of that punitive sporting tradition. For many country people, shooting was a lifelong passion, as were fox-, stag- and otter-hunting. I spent the years from when I could first run wild, perhaps six or seven – long before I had a gun – until my late teens, happily wandering through woods and fields watching animals being killed or, later, chasing and killing them myself. The rules were straightforward and unchallenged, a country apartheid every bit as uncompromising and odious as its human counterpart. With the exception of small birds, wildlife was either game or vermin, white or black, as stark and uncompromising as that. And yet, curiously and counter-intuitively, it was also both traditional and fashionable for country people, particularly those with leisure time to fill, folk who would then have described themselves as gentry, to study natural history. Many were serious, and seriously good amateur naturalists. Immaculately arranged collections of birds' eggs, butterflies, beetles and pressed flowers were commonplace, even the norm – and there were rules: an intriguing code of moral and ethical standards by which you operated your collections.

Never take more than one egg from a nest; only one rare orchid to be pressed. Never attempt to pin out your butterfly, moth or your beetle until you were quite sure it was dead in the killing bottle. As children we were taught how to fold and crush laurel leaves with a rolling pin and place them in the killing jar. Their aromatic vapours overpowered the butterflies quickly, but the beetles took much longer. If you removed them too quickly they came back to life. I am still troubled by the image of a stag beetle going nowhere, swimming on a pin hours after I had impaled it.

The library shelves in my childhood home contained many exquisitely illustrated volumes of bird books, wild flower guides, encyclopaedias of natural history, guides to butterflies and moths, fungi, and even one I remember on injurious insects – stinging and biting flies and wasps. They were old and foxed and smelt fusty, but the illustrations were often protected by thin veils of tissue, to be lifted carefully aside so that the delicate watercolour prints were revealed in their full glory. It was from these precious early tomes that I garnered so much inspiration to discover wild nature for myself.

Not until much later did it dawn on me that the paradox

of killing the things you admired so much that you wanted to keep them was one of the perplexing contradictions of serious nature study of the day. This, coupled with obsessive and lyrical adulation of game species in art, prose, poetry and taxidermy, while lustily chasing otters, foxes, deer and hares and wilfully exhorting the extermination of most hooked beaks and carnivores, seemed at the time entirely rational and unremarkable. The two omissions from the list were rabbits and badgers. Rabbits were widely shot, trapped, netted and snared by all country people and formed a staple in their diet, and badger digging and baiting was a pastime – a sport, even – and the common preserve of village boys with time on their hands.

There was no excuse. It is no good trying to blame the confused standards of the times or my upbringing. I knew that my grandfather loved birds. He knew not only his robins from his wrens, but also his redpolls from his redwings, and his notes scribbled in pencil in the margins of some of those books are testament to where he had seen them, and to his lifelong interest in all country things. I also knew very well that having an owl in that old yew was a joy to him; it was a symbol of continuity, of English village country life going on as it had done for many centuries. That much had been made endearingly clear to me from his tone. The three of them had seemed to me to fit together in an ageless trinity of absolute belonging. He loved the tree for its antiquity and its long association with owls and he loved the owl for the refinement with which its occupation graced the tree. He certainly knew that tawny owls did no harm to anyone.

For all his exploits with the gun, I am sure he never shot an owl; nor would he have condoned it by a gamekeeper, far less his grandson.

The head-hanging truth that still torments my soul is that when no one was looking I crept out and shot that owl. For a moment it seemed not to move; then it tipped forward and fell like a rag at my feet. I picked it up, hot and floppy in my hands. Its cinnamon and cream mottled plumage was as soft and silky as Angora fleece. One owl, one boy, one gun. Two burst hearts, one with lead, the other with guilt. I had never held a tawny owl before and its lifeless beauty hit me in a withering avalanche of instantaneous remorse and shame. I have never forgotten it and never forgiven myself.

To this day I ask myself why I did it. Was it the raw, puerile stupidity of vandalism, or did some uninvited surge of pre-pubescent carnal machismo wade in and take over, blinding what little formative judgement I possessed? I don't know; but I do know that it was to become one of the definitive climacterics of my adolescence. At that moment something indefinable inside me changed, like a pupal case splitting open to reveal the real insect. It wasn't just shame: it was a deeper, purer catharsis, like snapping out of hypnosis and awaking to see the real world around me for the first time.

I hid the corpse under leaves deep in a thicket and never told a soul. But, like Lady Macbeth's damned spot, the image of the dead owl in my hand refused to go away. It haunted me then and it haunts me still. Although I went on to enjoy game shooting as a social convention for many years, from that day forward, in the hope that it might assuage my guilt,

I adhered to the sporting doctrine of 'A Father's Advice' with the purity of the Absolute.

Later, in my teens, I reared tawny owlets that had been gusted prematurely from their nests while in the flightless, fluffy-tennis-ball stage. I have forgotten how many, but certainly five or six over as many years. I loved them all, but releasing them successfully to the wild became a passionate plea for absolution and atonement, an expiation demanded by the immortal owl within. It may also be that that one event, that single dead owl in my hand, conspired to bring about two important changes in my life, the second maturing from the first: one, that I determined to know and understand as much about nature as I could; and two, that in the fullness of maturity, I would become a lifelong, committed nature conservationist.

\*   \*   \*

I still can't be trusted with owls. Not that any of the four species we have around us at Aigas need fear. It's just that I can't be trusted to pass them by. They are more likely to get to know me as the shadowy figure with binoculars round his neck standing unobtrusively under a tree in the hope of witnessing the silken mystery of their mesmerising flight. My problem is that I have come to identify with them so powerfully that I can no longer deny them or even the thought of them. If I see an owl I have to abandon what I'm doing and all my attention is sapped until it's gone. If I find one dead at the roadside I suffer the leaden-winged burden of doom.

We have the ubiquitous tawnies with us all the time. We hear their hooting and shrieking calls, and delight in their silent, wafting glides from tree to tree. It is one of the moonlit nocturnes of winter at Aigas that I look forward to every year.

In a pause between gales the full moon arose, still, stark, and as pale as a white peach. In the small hours of that cool February morning I lay and watched the mercurial light slide silently across the bedroom ceiling. Tawny owls were calling in the woods below the loch. They seemed to be responding to the brilliance of the moon.

I was drowsily building a mental picture of them clashing over territorial claims in the run-up to mating when one bird came close; it must have flown soundlessly to the big ash tree that stands at the south-west corner of the house, only twenty yards from my bedroom window. It hooted so loudly and so unexpectedly that I started and was instantly wide awake. I jumped out of bed and stood at the casement staring out into the monochrome night.

Another long, wavering note, round and wooden and cavernous, pitched somewhere between an oboe and a bassoon, primed the night air with a strangely disturbing metaphysical quality of wildness. I followed the sound and, to my delight, on the edge of a lattice of naked ash branches the owl was immaculately silhouetted against the moon; a small, compact oval like a Russian doll, perched on an outer branch on my side of the tree. Through the binoculars I keep at my bedside I could see it perfectly, even the moon-shine reflected in its large round eyes as its head swivelled enquiringly from side to side. It called again, so distinct and direct that it seemed personal, a call to me alone, like a summons from another world. I could even see the mist of its hot breath. I determined to try to understand tawny calls.

*       *       *

Tawny owls have a variety of calls, but typically it is the 't-wit-t-woo' of nursery rhymes that wrongly stereotypes them together. The 't-wit' is more properly a harsh, pene-trating two-syllabled 'kvi-ik', often repeated over and over again, and may signal communication as well as a challenge to would-be invaders, and the 't-woo' is the long, wobbling, drawn out hoo-oo-oot it is so easy to mimic by blowing into your cupped hands. Both sexes are thought to be capable of making both calls, although the books will tell you that the males typically hoo-oot and the females kvi-ik.

Mike Thom, the British ornithologist who probably knows more about owls than anyone else alive, tells me that 'While generally the male owl is the more vocal of the two sexes, advertising his territory, females often produce calls of their own and will sometimes "duet" with their mate. The familiar "hooo hu huhuhuhooo" call of the male, for example, is often answered by the female with a "keewik" contact call, this sometimes overlapping with the end note of the male's call. Females sometimes produce a similar call to the male's hoot, though it is higher in pitch, coarser in nature and with less precise phrasing.'

*       *       *

Somewhere out there, silent and secretive, is a pair of long-eared owls. We almost never see them. The western red cedars, planted in clumps 130 years ago and constantly spreading outwards by the furtive process of branches layering wherever they touch the ground, are now dark jungles of evergreen foliage on the outside, and impenetrable grottoes of dead branches and dark trunks looming up into the lofty canopy on the inside. They create perfect asylums for fell deeds and skulking beasts. A young male badger recently took up residence in a shallow dugout under the buttress roots of one massive stem. He had probably been ousted from his clan by a more dominant male and found a temporary home for himself under our trees. Roe deer sometimes lie up in these thickets, and pine martens and foxes slink in there to devour their filched chickens.

High above them, silently watching from a lofty perch, are the long-eared owls. This beautiful owl, with feather tufts (which aren't ears at all), like extended eyebrows, reaching an inch above its head, is one of my problem birds. Every spring I search for them and mostly I fail to find them, although I do occasionally hear their deep, booming calls in the dead of night. In recent years I have seen only one, killed by a peregrine or a goshawk, stripped bare to the breast keel, lying on its back with spread wings on the heather moor. Whenever I have found their nest in the past it has always been because I have tracked down the unmistakable 'squeaking-gate' calls of the young. It is thought that they are universally in decline in the UK because of competition by tawnies. I haven't found a nest for a few years now and if I don't find another soon I shall begin to worry that ours have also been squeezed out.

Their diurnal cousin of the same genus, *Asio*, the short-eared owl, with barely visible 'ear' tufts, but which might better be called the long-winged owl (it has the longest wings of any British owl), is much easier to see. It wafts along the riverbank and across the marshes with slow, rowing down-beats, wavering glides and side-slips, more like a harrier than an owl. I used to see them regularly from my study window, a sight that always brought me to my feet, whatever I was doing, and still does, but less often now that agriculture has purified the pastures with Italian rye grass leys and the irre-pressible craze for silage, so devastating to partridges, corn-crakes, corn buntings and lapwings, as well as an unsung and unknown host of invertebrates. Even the once ubiqui-tous yellowhammers have given up and gone away.

It is a very confiding owl. If I stand still at the field edge it will hunt right up to and past me, sometimes perching on a fence post to quiz me from bright yellow eyes set in a bulging disc, giving it a slightly foolish look with an unnerving, baleful expression. Grouse-moor owners and their keepers confuse this bird with the hen harrier for being a grouse-chick predator, which it probably only rarely is, although it does favour heather moorland. Its breeding success depends entirely on the abundance of voles. There is no doubt that both species are still quietly removed by keepers, an illegal persecution it is extremely difficult to prove or to stop.

That leaves the barn owl, sometimes called the screech

owl, one of the world's most numerous and successful owl species. Viewed globally and numerically, the barn owl is a bird of the tropics and sub-tropics, much aided by the presence of people, with whom there seems to have been a close association for uncounted thousands of years. Wherever we go rodents follow: rats, mice and voles in particular. Barn owls are principally rodent predators, although they are capable of catching a much wider variety of prey. The consequence of our rodent followers is that barn owls have moved in too: church belfries, ruins, cow sheds and, of course, barns. We are lucky to have them at Aigas: we are close to the most northerly reaches of their range.

Ours have chosen to nest in an entirely natural site, a rock hole in the face of the disused quarry a mile away, and they hunt the river fields at dusk. I know of no bird whose ghostly presence engages with the human spirit as profoundly and vividly as that of the barn owl. The freckled golden mantle, the heart-shaped face, the dark, penetrating eyes and the luminous white under-wings as it floats silently through the dusk, all combine to give this hauntingly beautiful creature an ethereal, almost mystical quality that can be both disturbing and unforgettable.

My association with barn owls began not long after I shot the tawny, but mercifully unburdened by guilt. I found one in an old red-brick barn in the middle of a corn field. It was sick and I never knew why. When I approached it on the barn floor it made no attempt to fly or move away. It appeared unharmed but was thin and listless. I took it home and tried to feed it with strips of raw meat. It was the time when the agricultural world was rejoicing at the 'miracle' of the DDT pesticide. I suspect it was a victim of secondary poisoning. It died that night.

Faced with a corpse, I examined it carefully. Snowy white belly and underwings; golden mottled mantle, back and tops to the wings; snow-white face fringed in a filigree of tiny gold feathers; large, forward-facing eyes as black and shiny as wet coal; long white legs and scimitar talons sharper than fish-hooks; a short, button-hook bill with whiskery white feathers peaked forward between the eyes, like a nose. And those wing feathers. I had read about the silent flight of owls and now I could see why. The edge of each feather was gossamer thin and as fine and soft as thistledown. I was entranced.

It so happened that an aged schoolmaster cousin had recently visited my parents and brought some cured duck skins to show me. 'It's easy,' he assured me, handing over an extremely sad-looking gadwall that appeared to have been run over. 'Once you've skinned it, treat it with borax and dry it thoroughly. It will keep for ever.' I did as he instructed with my owl and it seemed to work. It lived carefully folded in tissue paper in a box in my bedroom along with many other natural-history trophies. But he had failed to warn me about feather mites and that all museum collections treated their skins with an arsenic paste. One day a year later I opened the box to find my barn owl in tatters. I was aghast. Most of it had been consumed, shredded to dust by these silent, unseen vandals. I wrote off my first attempt at preserving a bird skin as a disaster; I would not make the same mistake again. But its magic had worked. I had held a barn owl in my hands and knew its startling beauty in life and in death.

★　　★　　★

Nature writers are supposed to be able to summon from the literary ether the precise words to describe their subjects or the feelings they evince. Sometimes the Muse attends, but by no means on demand. It is one of the great delights of trying to be a writer that words can suddenly appear, like the blackcap's jubilant song, absent for months and then unexpectedly and ecstatically there, winging into your head just when you need them most. The more emotive the subject or the more deeply personal the experience, the easier it ought to be. But not necessarily so. Some experiences transcend ready description as though making a point: words – at least those available to the generality of writers – sometimes fall hopelessly short; they dish out despair in bucket loads. Others fare much better.

John Alec Baker, the shy, almost reclusive 1960s author of *The Peregrine* and *The Hill of Summer*, is often cited as the modern gold standard for lyrical nature writing. I know of very few naturalists and nature writers of my generation who have not been influenced by his work. I freely own up to that. Not only have I never viewed nature writing in the same light after reading him, but I have never viewed a peregrine falcon without his luminous descriptions zooming in and taking over. Of a short-eared owl he wrote:

Heavy clouds lowered, and the afternoon was dull. Mustard yellow in the dusky light, a short-eared owl rose silently from a ditch, floated up like a buoyant moon, with no sound but the soft rustle of the parting grass. Turning its cat-like face towards me, it flexed its mottled snakeskin wings across the marsh.

And so it is that I have struggled to find the right words to do justice to the barn owl and its flight, something I have so often seen, that has been with me since boyhood, but which never fails to stop me dead in my tracks, make me hold my breath. I believe it is one of those experiences one has to witness to understand properly. It's personal. Unashamedly, I went searching for help.

First I turned to some of the 'greats' of twentieth-century ornithology. Messrs Witherby, Jourdain, Ticehurst and Tucker's *Handbook of British Birds*, first published in 1942, which would become the standard work for the following thirty-five years and was the first bird reference book I knew well. One of my earliest memories is of my father poring over its five volumes. They say of the white-breasted barn owl (there are at least two distinct races):

> . . . seen on the wing as ghostly, whitish form in dusk . . . but also on winter afternoons . . . when pale appearance with orange-buff upper parts, pure white face and underparts, equally attracts the eye, as it quarters ground with buoyant, wavering flight and . . . pounces down to seize a mouse or vole.

This was a promising start – good, accurate in a clipped, academic orthodoxy – but not really what I was looking for.

Thence to the rather grander and much more conversational Bannerman and Lodge, *The Birds of the British Isles*, 1955, in twelve volumes, with its fine watercolour illustrations by George Lodge, but despite its long and detailed essay on barn owls, the authors seemed to be unmoved by the bird: 'When seen, as is most probable, this owl appears almost white in the evening light.'

Undeterred by this prosaic dismissal, I turned to W. Swaysland's *Familiar Wild Birds* of 1888. But things got worse. Mr Swaysland plunges into a dismally critical view that can only suggest to me that he had never watched barn owls in person: 'The flight of the Owl is dull and heavy, but particularly noiseless.'

I was beginning to despair when the Rev. F. O. Morris's *Morris's British Birds*, 4th edition of 1895, came to my rescue. Perhaps, after all, I wasn't alone in my exultation over this bird. Like Richard Jefferies, Morris refers to them as 'white owls', then helpfully lists their alternative local names: 'yellow owl, screech owl, gilli-howlet, church owl and hissing owl'. A little later in his rather disjointed description, as much about taming owls as observing them, he ignites the flame:

> The flight of this bird, which is generally low, is pre-eminently soft, noiseless and volatile. It displays considerable agility on the wing, and may be seen in the tranquil summer evening when prowling about, turning backward and forward over a

limited extent of beat, as if trained to hunt, as indeed it has been – by Nature.

Quite so. And then he rounds off his piece with a verse from Thomas Gray's famous 'Elegy Written in a Country Churchyard':

> Save that from yonder ivy-mantled tower
> The moping owl doth to the moon complain
> Of such, as wandering near her sacred bower
> Molest her ancient solitary reign.

So far so good. By now I was happy to have confirmed that some people shared my Romantic enthusiasm for this soft-plumed creature of the dusk. But I was still searching for something more intimate, more personal, something that touched my soul, as did the bird every time I saw it. I scoured even more ancient tomes, such as Robert Mudie's *The Feathered Tribes of the British Islands*, 1834, but for all its delightfully quaint phraseology, it was to no real avail, except that in his revealing '. . . stands not accused . . .' line he provides further affirmation that in the nineteenth century other owls were not just incorrectly accused but also heavily persecuted for taking game:

This is the most common, the most familiar, the most useful, and in its plumage perhaps the most beautiful of all the British owls. Instead of spurning the society of man, it courts the neighbourhood of his dwelling; and while it is more destructive of mice, in all their species, barn, field and bank, than any of the other owls, it stands not accused of destroying any sort of game . . . It does not skin its mice, but breaks the bones, and returns these and other indigestible parts in pellets . . .

If only Robert Mudie's view had held true for the Victorian era, but, writing forty-five years later, Richard Jefferies not only finds the barn-owl carcasses gibbeted with all the others but endorses the point: 'The barn owls are more liable to be shot because they are more conspicuous.'

★    ★    ★

Nowadays the Aigas rangers collect barn-owl pellets from underneath the quarry nest site. They bring them back to our little environmental education centre in polythene bags and offer them to classes of schoolchildren to dissect. This rather messy process involves soaking the pellet in water in a tray and gently teasing it apart with a probe and forceps, floating off the hair and unravelling the bones. Each pellet is a bundle of tightly packed fur, bones, teeth and skulls of prey, evicted from the crop with a series of rather undignified hiccups. Most predatory birds regurgitate indigestible detritus this way.

In this glen our barn owls are principally feeding on wood mice and field voles with a few beetles and shrews snapped up for a change of flavour, but in the process of teasing pellets apart there is always the exciting possibility of something really unusual, such as a pipistrelle bat's skull or a lizard's toes and claws or the cartilaginous sections of a slow worm's spine.

The children work in twos. They pore over the trays, initially expressing disgust but quickly moving on to shrieks of 'Yeah! Cool!' as another tiny skull emerges from the murky water and, matched to the key, proves to be of the predicted species. Later they glue their washed prizes to a sheet of card, grouping together the voles and the mice, with the unusual extras highlighted in shocking pink or lime green – 'We got a frog in ours!' – building a chart of successful hunting that can be compared with the findings from other dissected pellets. It becomes highly competitive, much jostling and calling for the rangers' approval of their handiwork.

Cornish artist Alastair Mackie has chosen the unlikely medium of mouse skulls found in barn-owl pellets from a disused building on his family farm with which to pursue his theme of 'Metamorphoses'. He collected hundreds of these skulls, cleaned them and reassembled them in a perfect sphere. When I first stumbled across this astonishing artwork in a Devon gallery, I couldn't believe the skulls were real. I thought he had re-created them in moulded white plastic and I was about to dismiss it as a piece of imaginative gimmickry when, on a closer look, and having often pored over pellet dissection myself, I saw that they were indeed the real thing: many hundreds of mouse skulls, every one slightly different, all facing upwards, but perfectly cleaned and intricately assembled into this hollow, small football-sized perfect sphere representing, I imagine, Mother Earth.

It reminded me of the art of minuscule Chinese ivory carving, but whereas I cannot look at any ivory without picturing the tragic destruction of elephants, this mouse-cranial orb, to me as a naturalist, was a dazzlingly imaginative reaffirmation of the interdependence of all living things. I treasured the image, hoarding it away as one of the most delicate and captivating works of creative art I had ever seen. The catalogue said that he 'had traced the "states of being" of one creature absorbed by another and reconfigured into a work of art'. He certainly had.

★   ★   ★

Back in the winter of 2009–10 when more than a foot of snow lay for three months and temperatures crashed to –18° Celsius, with the grim inevitability of being a top predator, our barn owls starved. Voles and mice can survive happily under snow for weeks on end, their maze of tunnels, latrines and food caches eventually exposed by a thaw. But their security means that the owls' pale nightly vigils around the fields are fruitless. The marshes and the loch were gripped white with frost, the Beauly Firth froze over so that the tide floated sheets of salt ice onto the foreshore, heaped like rime-covered slates from a fallen roof, preventing the owls from hunting even there.

That spring, when finally it came, I took Alicia, one of our young rangers, down to the quarry to see if there was any sign of our only local breeding pair of barn owls. As we clambered through the winter-burned rushes towards the rock face I saw something white up ahead. My heart sank. I knew very well what it was.

On its back with wings outstretched lay the emaciated corpse of a barn owl. I picked it up. It weighed nothing, a feathered wraith of the once vibrant bird. It was withered and dry; talons clenched in a final, defiant clutch against mortality. It had been dead for weeks, fallen from the sky as it struggled back to the sanctuary of its nest site – perhaps the place where it was born. Its eyes were sunken hollows in the soft, golden fringed heart of its face. I handed it to Alicia. 'Damn,' I whispered. 'I was afraid we might find this.' When I looked at her again, tears were running down her cheeks.

A few weeks ago, browsing one evening at my fireside, I found, perhaps where I should have looked first, in my old friend Richard Mabey's *Nature Cure* (2005), an evocation of exactly what had inspired to me to love barn owls all those decades ago:

> The memory of the owls beating past the poplar trees – burnished golden wings against lime-green in the evening light – is one of the few visual images of childhood I can recall with absolute clarity . . . Few birds are so dramatically beautiful, or can bring the exquisite delicacy of flight so close to us, or can look at us so penetratingly, eye to eye.

# II

# The Long Wait

When Springtime came, red Robin built a nest,
And trilled a lover's song in sheer delight.
Grey hoarfrost vanished, and the Rose with might
Clothed her in leaves and buds of crimson core.

'A Wintry Sonnet', Christina Rossetti

It is the second week of February before our latitude hands us back a full working day. After months of getting up in the dark and having to abandon outdoor work early, it's revitalising to find that once again there is a full eight hours of daylight. Our woodland edges are the first to test winter's mettle. In radiant drifts of white, snowdrops are blooming defiantly among quilts of snow-flattened leaves. If it happens that the temperature is generous, as it has been of late, the small resident birds – tits, robins, wrens – seem to adopt the mood, and the woods suddenly resound with rasping, sawing, trilling song.

Yet for all those tantalising enticements, this is the most frustrating moment of the year. Those with sense go away, take a break, skip south to the sun, as we have done many times. It helps to discard a chunk of February like that. To stay is to trudge through the long, depressing wait for the

Highland spring, still fully two months away. But what is even more frustrating is knowing that in southern England daffodils are blooming and birds are nesting. Here the spring fools with us like a child with a puppy on a long lead, letting it go and then hauling it back in.

Yes, the days go on getting reliably longer, and the sun continues to inch its way up the sky, but for every day that seems a little warmer and brighter, there are two or three that drag us back to winter. Sleet and icy rain on snarling winds, cheek-stinging hail squalls, swingeing frosts and sudden snowfalls are all entirely predictable throughout the whole of March and well into April. While smiling southerners are busy oiling their lawnmowers, we are still grimly longing for the daffodils to burst.

I am a Taurean. My birthday falls in the second week of May and I use it to gauge the season every year. Downy birch, *Betula pubescens* (often wrongly but forgivably called silver birch), is our commonest native Highland tree. It loves acid soils and, with enviable stoicism, is wholly unfazed by our increasingly capricious climate. Ignoring the cold and wet, it grows vigorously wherever its delicate wind-borne seed flutters into a niche. Some years the first birch leaf appears in late April, others it is the first few days of May, but occasionally, if it has been held back by desiccating cold winds, green tips are only just showing on the eighth.

Snow can arrive at any time. Often I have awakened on my birthday to find the world white with a dusting of fresh snow, and the local crofters always shake their heads sagely and warn me, 'Aye, that'll be the lambing storm. There could be more yet.'

It seems perverse, but it's so often the case that just as the first lambs on wobbly legs are beginning to appear in the fields up and down the glen, usually around Easter, the snow comes barrelling through with an overnight dump sometimes several inches deep. Every now and again I have to remind myself that I have chosen to live north of the 57th parallel, closer to the Faroe Islands than to London, closer to the Arctic Circle than to Paris – something the Arctic's icy tendrils never let us forget.

So spring comes late to the Highlands – always. It is what history tells us to expect. My neighbour Finlay Macrae, whose crofting family have eked an agricultural existence from these acid soils for more generations than he can remember, assures me with a grin beaming across wind-tanned cheeks, that the grass in his wet and rushy river meadows doesn't really start growing until the second week of June – growing, that is, sufficient for his out-wintered cattle to get their tongues around it.

Reading Dr Isabel F. Grant, the universally respected early-twentieth-century historian of Highland life, in her book *Everyday Life on an Old Highland Farm 1769–82*, a low point in history for the Highlands and a period of near-starvation for many Highland cottars, I learn that the menfolk had physically to carry their cows out of the byres onto the fresh grass at the end of winter because they were so weak after six months indoors on minimal feed.

Nowadays, of course, in the age of silage and the big round

bale, farmers, small-holders and crofters have sophisticated methods for harvesting and storing winter feed, so that animals can be kept and even fattened during the long winter months. Back then, when the only winter feed was hay and a few soggy turnips from a clamp, and when a wet summer turned a bad hay crop mouldy, the cattle scraped a similarly grim existence to that of their impoverished owners.

Wildlife has always had to take pot luck. If times are good, most wild animals do well, but when the weather turns sour and food supplies fail, they suffer and fail too. That is the process by which natural selection has honed them for survival over millions of years. Populations build and then they crash. The survivors are the ones who go on to breed tougher, stronger, more adaptable offspring and populations begin to claw their way up again.

The word Charles Darwin made famous is 'fittest' – the survival of the fittest – to which he added his visionary quotation: 'It is not the strongest of the species that survives, nor the most intelligent that survives. It is the one that is the most adaptable to change.' In the context of change, the word 'fittest' means those species most able to adapt their behaviour or their feeding and breeding habits at the same pace as the change – whatever that change may be – is affecting them. Some change will bring benefits. Other changes will severely disadvantage them.

A bird laying eggs expects and needs to be able to feed its chicks. If it is pinned by evolution to a particular food supply, and suddenly that food is removed or delayed, or even reduced in quantity or quality, and the bird finds it cannot feed its chicks, they will die. Newly hatched chicks of every species have an extremely rapid metabolism, requiring a constant input of energy. If they don't get it, they will die very quickly, within a matter of hours if they don't receive the quantity and type of food they need. It doesn't matter whether it is a blue tit, a golden eagle or a mallard duck, it's tough out there: they have no reserves, so they perish. The adults have to have a mechanism by which they can cope with change and try again. Many bird species are programmed to accept failure by starvation or predation and simply lay more eggs next time round.

A few years ago a pair of robins nested in a yew stump three feet off the ground. I watched the nest daily and counted the eggs when the hen flew off to feed. When she had six a predator – I suspected a weasel, a rat or a stoat – raided the nest. The adults escaped, but the entire clutch vanished. For three days they sat about, looking bewildered. Then, to my delight and surprise, they began building a new nest only ten feet away from the previous one. I worried that the same predator was also watching and would strike again, but I was wrong. The new nest, an elaborate mossy cup lined with sheep's wool, took them less than a week to complete; then she started to lay again. Did the robins know what they were doing or was it just luck? Who knows? It doesn't matter; the important point is that it worked. Robins have adapted. They have a mechanism for surviving raids like that one. This time she went on to raise seven chicks.

★　　★　　★

Darwin carefully used all-embracing terms, like 'fittest' and 'change', words that cover a multiplicity of complex vicissitudes. In these puzzling times it is climate change that is exercising me. We know it is happening – there seems to be plenty of evidence for that – but we cannot yet determine its pace or its permanence. Neither do we know the fullest implications or consequences to ourselves or to wildlife, no matter how adaptable that wildlife has become.

Only a few years ago 'global warming' was the catchphrase for environmental alarm. There is little doubt that greenhouse gases, especially methane and carbon dioxide, are contributing to the gradual rise in temperature across the globe. There seems to be little we can do about it in the short term, but because the places apparently suffering most from rising temperatures are the extremes – the Arctic and Antarctic polar ice, places too far away actually to impact on our collective imagination – the new emphasis of alarm has shifted to something undisputedly evident in our own backyards: climate change.

And it is alarm with good cause. Rapid climate change is scary. Ecologists are very gloomy about the Arctic ice cap, and the prospects for the polar bear as a pack-ice, seal-hunting top predator; but far closer to home, for most of us in the extravagant West, over the past few decades global warming has manifested itself in sudden and unwelcome bursts of extreme weather: floods, hurricanes and storms, droughts and blizzards. We plunge from hosepipe bans to widespread flooding and consequential landslides, not just in one year but in one summer. Winters have their own grim signature:

white-out blizzards bringing traffic to a standstill one minute, storm-force winds and lashing rain, power cuts, flooding and tidal surges the next.

For many the words 'climate change' have come to mean discomfort, disruption, financial loss, despair, anxiety and stress – even life-threatening events. Right now, at the time of writing only a few days before Easter 2013, most of the west of Britain and Northern Ireland is at a standstill with blizzards, and the people on the island of Arran, off south-west Scotland, are struggling with snowdrifts up to fourteen feet deep and have been without power for a week, a situation unprecedented in living memory. No one knows where or when such extremes will strike next.

We have no choice but to speculate and hope for the best, as must so many of the species, plant and animal, with which we share our planet. Powerless, we watch and, hopefully, we learn. It's like a game of roulette we've been sucked into against our will, forced to gamble. For us, we bet on our jobs, our livelihoods, our homes, our standards of living. And, when made to, we adapt: we move, we build flood defences, we duck and weave, we adjust, we change our habits. For wildlife it's much tougher; only an adaptable few can change quickly. They toss their genes into the wheel and see how they fare. Red is good and they can adapt; black is death, if not immediately then a gradual decline into oblivion. If their number fails to come up there are no consolation prizes.

Change can mean shifts in predation too. Our eight-acre loch at Aigas used to have moorhens and coot, little grebes, teal, mallard and wigeon all ground-nesting in the woods or on the marsh and sedges around its shores. They did well, despite regular nest predation on land by a formidable array of predators: foxes, pine martens, wildcats, buzzards, herons and hoodie crows. Once they got their chicks onto the water they did well. Then mink arrived – alien American mink that had escaped or been released from mink-fur farms. Mink are voracious and relentless predators, as much at home in water as on land. Suddenly we lost our ground-nesting birds at the loch – and not just some: we lost the lot, except one tough old species, the mallard duck. One by one the other species disappeared. They couldn't change their habits and behaviour quickly enough to cope with this new, extra layer of predation on land and in the water. Mallard are a famously resilient and successful species right across the northern hemisphere. They nest on the ground. If the nest is discovered by one of those many egg predators (the list is startling: gulls, crows, herons, rats, stoats, weasels, foxes, hedgehogs, badgers, otters, pine martens, mink . . .) the mallard loses the lot. But the success of the mallard as a species is precisely because it is so adaptable.

As a general rule, the more successful the species the more adaptable it proves to be. In Britain, think house sparrows, herring gulls, the crow family, wood pigeons, chaffinches, blackbirds, herons and many more common species. In every case they can move easily from habitat to habitat, from food supply to food supply, from nest site to nest site. They cope with whatever man throws at them and they keep coming back for more. Adaptability is their byword.

The mallard is an excellent exemplar: defence adaptation number one is the camouflaged plumage of the duck and her ability to freeze. I have stepped on a nesting mallard before she flew up. Number two is the wide diversity of habitats in which she can nest: woods, marshes, fields, scrub and thickets, in gardens, up against walls, in old hollow logs, in drifts of leaves . . . The list goes on and on. Many species are tied to one particular habitat. Not so the mallard, and she will learn by harsh experience which nesting sites are successful and which to avoid. Adaptation number three is her cunning laying technique. She can lay only one egg per day, so she lays it in her carefully prepared nest and covers it with down. Then she heads back to the water and safety. She doesn't return to the nest until she's ready to drop another egg, thereby keeping her presence at the nest to an absolute minimum. She keeps this up for as long as three weeks, sometimes laying as many as fifteen eggs. During that time her giveaway presence at the nest has been absolutely minimal, a few hours only, every time carefully covering the clutch with down from her own breast, then with grass and leaves. But that's not the end of it. Adaptation number four is another cunning ploy. For the safety of her chicks it is vital that they all hatch together, within a matter of an hour or two, so that she can lead them to water together (we have all witnessed the endearing sight of a mother leading them across a main road). So, once the clutch is complete, she covers it up, then abandons it to allow all the eggs to cool to exactly the same temperature. This ensures that none of them starts to develop until she brings them back up to 37.5° Celsius. She can leave them for as long as three weeks before returning to begin incubation. This secret hoard of concealed eggs, if undiscovered, must mean there is no trace of duck scent emanating from the eggs, or anywhere near the nest. She sneaks back in, settles, bares her brood patches and begins the long twenty-eight-day incubation. If she has to leave the nest she covers it over again and is away for the shortest time she can to keep herself fed and watered. Adaptation number five is her ability, apparently unfazed by losing an entire clutch of eggs first time round, to find another site and, within a few weeks, build a new nest and lay another clutch. The same thing could happen several times, but mallard ducks don't give up. Despite being hit over and over again by predators, eventually she will raise a duckling or two to replace herself. But the trump card she has, adaptation number six, is not just her laudable and obstinate refusal to give up (it breaks my heart to see a clutch of twelve ducklings successfully hatched and, within a few hours, down to eight, then to five, and finally one if it's lucky), it is her longevity.

In captivity mallard have survived in breeding condition for twenty years. In the hazardous wild it is likely to be much less, but assuming an average lifespan of only eight years, during that time a duck can produce hundreds of ducklings. Even though only one or two may survive each year, if she herself survives, by the time she succumbs she may well have replaced herself and her mate many times over.

Other species can't do that. Wrens and other small birds,

such as tits, live for only two or three years, so they have to have another trick – that of extra-large, multiple broods. If wrens have been hit by a hard winter, which they often are, suffering as much as 60 per cent losses – tiny bodies can't maintain their heat in long periods of sub-zero – the survivors are well known to take up the challenge of rescuing the species by producing up to twice the size of egg clutch, from a norm of five or six eggs to ten or eleven, then repeating it a few weeks later. Wrens in particular seem to know that they will die in extreme cold so they gang together in tight spaces for mutual body warmth. There have been some remarkable instances of dozens of wrens all jammed together in nest boxes. The British Trust for Ornithology cites the record number of wrens roosting together in one box to be sixty-three, but the RSPB lists a record of ninety-eight wrens emerging from one hole in an attic. The largest I have found was twenty-one, in the extreme winter of 1998, all jammed together in a tit nest box. The nail had rusted through and the box fell to earth. A dead wren lay beside it. When I lifted the lid and looked inside I was astonished to find what I took to be another twenty dead wrens. I was horrified. I tipped them out onto a tray, then noticed a slight movement. A single leg stirred. They weren't dead, but comatose with cold. I put them in the Aga warming oven and brought them back to life. When they had completely recovered I released them again and nailed the box back onto its tree. Two nights later all twenty were back in the box. It had worked for them once, why not again?

Yet all these commonplace survival tricks that have evolved

over many hundreds of millennia, perhaps even millions of years, to enable species to fit the climate and habitat available to them, all have to submit to the caveat 'if everything else is equal', by which I mean on the assumption that the species in question has sufficient food to feed itself and its offspring. Jenny Wren can produce as many extra-large clutches as she likes, but if there is no food for her chicks, they are all doomed within hours of hatching. Similarly, if there are no insects on the water or in the marsh for the ducklings to eat in the first week of life, the mallard has no hope of raising even one duckling. That is what makes rapid climate change so scary – as we would discover, there's nothing 'equal' about it.

★   ★   ★

What was happening around us in the early spring was the beginning of a catastrophic inequality. An unforeseen factor was about to shoulder its way in to complicate the lives of just about everything around us. February had been dry and cold – nothing so unusual about that. The rooks came and went, checking things out, ready to pitch into nesting as soon as the conditions were right. By March everything looked good. Every day the sun rose with renewed determination and with it, as though to urge it on, came an unusually warm southerly breeze. It was gentle at first, delicious and, oh, so welcome. The rooks revelled in it, cawing incessantly as they busied back and forth around their bulging nests. Secateurs in hand, Lucy rushed out into the garden and vanished into a herbaceous border for hours at a stretch, stripping out the winter-killed stems of last autumn's blooms. I started the rounds of the many nest boxes on our trails, scribbling notes as I went. Great, blue and coal tits were all busy carrying filaments of moss and sheep's wool. It seemed we were 'set fair', as the barometer says.

Normally – and I can only really speak for the 'normality' of the last forty years – March in the Highlands is treacherous. It can be warm or icy, wet or dry, calm or stormy, through all of which the daffodils struggle valiantly into full bloom at last, and that splendid normality is leavened by the lifting sun supplying us with a broadly upward temperature trend zigzagging gently towards April. Years ago old Dunc Macrae, my crofting neighbour Finlay's father, now long dead, told me he never fussed about snow in March: 'Ach, it will na stay. It'll be away in a day or two.' Dunc's reassurance was unnecessary, the snow never came. It was the last thing on my mind. The long wait had taken its toll: I was sick of waiting, sick of winter. As far as I was concerned, spring had arrived. Now, along with just about everything else, I was enjoying the warmth.

# 12

# The Sun's Rough Kiss

These violent delights have violent ends
And in their triumph die, like fire and powder
Which, as they kiss, consume.

*Romeo and Juliet*, Act II, scene vi,
William Shakespeare

Looking back, we had no idea. It all seemed normal. February had surrendered to March without a fuss. Only the moon noticed the difference, off on its rounds again. Despite the first daffodils' most ecstatic fling, nobody round here expected March to be anything but another month of winter dragging its feet. Even April can hang in the balance, so in March we expected to wait on, patiently, trying hard to avoid the word 'spring', although the great tits were nagging and the wrens were taunting us all day long.

Frosts had crisped the lawn for the last two weeks of February and mists hung over the river until noon when, like a bolshie teenager, the sun seemed to wake up properly and managed a smile. It was good. Most days were dry. We were out and about, doing tasks we hadn't been able to do for months. Then, without warning, everything changed.

A gentle wind moseyed in, like a cruise ship docking from the Mediterranean, dragging with it a Continental high more appropriate to Monaco than the Moray Firth. It shimmied its glowing warmth up the whole of Britain. Overnight the clouds of our little wintry world vanished. There was no excuse for the sun now. March glowed and then it blazed. Average seasonal temperatures doubled from 10° to 20° Celsius and more. Records began to tumble. People rushed to the seaside and leaped into rivers and lakes. Camping shops sold out of tents. Three weeks later, as the month drew to a close, television news was reporting crazy temperatures: 23.6° Celsius at Aboyne, only an hour's eagle flight to the east of us in Aberdeenshire. The whole of March had been dry, most of it what us Brits like to call *hot*.

We loved it, of course. We strode about in shirtsleeves or none at all. We swam in the loch. The young field centre staff lay about sun-basking through their down time. A pensioner died from heat-stroke in Scarborough and no one seemed to care. We laughed and joked endlessly about summer, like most northern-hemisphere humans do when the sun shines for more than a day and a half. It was all jolly good fun. Every morning we awoke to a constantly expanding chorus of triumphant birdsong: chaffinches bellowing, woodpeckers drumming, robins carousing and wood pigeons, over and over again, calling out their soothing, summery instructions, 'Take two cows, Susan, take two cows.'

The rooks came home in force. Their nesting trees were a constant hubbub of domesticity. They carried in fresh sticks and set about rebuilding their twiggy piles with a perpetual racket of corvid commentary. They strode about the lawns as if they owned the place, drilling their gimlet bills into the turf, plucking unsuspecting leatherjackets into their hungry gullets. When we approached the paddock with a bucket of kitchen scraps for the hens, the rooks parachuted in like a pack of black vultures, lining the paddock fence in haggling gangs, loudly cawing their approval.

The first small tortoiseshell butterflies shook themselves free from hibernation, dancing prettily among daisy and dandelion blooms that suddenly studded the lawns, and queen wasps emerged from under the roof slates two months earlier than usual, droning slowly and purposefully in through bedroom windows thrown wide, diligently searching for secret hideaways to fashion their delicate little paper lanterns. It all seemed so good.

Brown hares deserted the woods and lolloped aimlessly about the fields, as if they couldn't quite believe the grass was growing. They cast nervously around, long, black-tipped ears ceaselessly swivelling and twitching with neurotic anxiety as though they oughtn't to be there at all. When they settled to graze, laying their ears back on their shoulder blades, through binoculars I could see their vibrating whiskers and curling, trembling lips taking each protein-laden growing point, hauling in each blade in turn.

Ears and eyes. That's what I love about hares. Those acutely honed senses, unsleeping ears, like satellite dishes, and big brown bulbous orbs set into the skull flanks for 170° vision on either side. That leaves twenty degrees of relative blindness, five to the front and fifteen at the back, for the ears to cover. An alerted rabbit just looks cheeky and mischievous, but the hare's glaucomatous eyes, bulging madly from a narrow, chiselled head full of sculpted hollows and angles, give it a look of crazed melancholy, whetted by perpetual terror. They remind me of a sensitive girl I once knew whose confidence had been terribly crushed by overweening parents.

> The March hare brings the spring
> For you personally.
> He is too drunk to deliver it.
> He loses it on some hare-brained folly –
> . . . All year he will be fleeing and flattening
> His ears and fleeing –
> Eluding your fury.
>
> 'Deceptions', *Season Songs*, Ted Hughes

I grew up with a print of Albrecht Dürer's meticulous hare drawing (1502) on my bedroom wall. It was mesmerising. As a small boy I stood and studied it intently. I wondered how he had got so close, how he had achieved so much vibrant detail from a living hare without the help of binoculars, detail that vanishes the moment the animal is dead. Did he just sit quietly with his sketch pad? Would they come close enough? It seemed unlikely. Did he have a tame hare or did he stalk his hares or use a hide? I decided to try for myself and I quickly found that stalking was not easy.

Hare-stalking is a game of great skill and no little

vexation. The best approach is from directly behind, but head-on can work too; from the side is hopeless. First, you have to slough off any thoughts of being human, hunker down into your careless senses and engage with the hare's own animal magnetism, with its force field of twitchy hyper-sentience, blocking everything else out. Wait until the head is down and grazing; be ready to freeze when the ears swivel to your direction or the head suddenly jerks up, which it will at intervals, regardless of whether it has detected you or not. Scent is important too: you must approach down-wind; gauge it on the tip of your tongue. Stick to cover until the last possible moment, and when you have to move out into the open imagine you are a tree. When you freeze don't look at the hare; fix on a point to one side of it and don't move your eyes.

It's Grandfather's Footsteps taken to the limits of human stealth, and a game the hare inevitably wins, flattening with the first hint of danger and freezing until its fear gets the better of it, then careening off at up to 70 m.p.h. On rare occasions I have got as close as ten yards, but at that range it's almost impossible for a human to move without making a hare-detectable sound.

*Lepus europaeus*, the brown hare, is a woodland animal and normally nocturnal, but gardens and fields of crops are often irresistible to them. I had seen none all winter but now the sunshine and the smell of new grass winkled them out of the woods. They gambolled and frolicked across the lawns in the dawn dew, adopting our mood, as excited about the radiant spring weather as the rest of us.

Buds began to explode. The birches, usually not leafed until the end of April, shimmered in a pastel haze. The horse chestnuts are always the first to leaf in spring and to colour up in autumn. They burst through their cinnamon sticky buds thrusting their five-to-seven-lobed leaflets into the sunlight as though they had something to prove. The avenue of balsam poplars hovered in a mist of heady scent, known as the Balm of Gilead, oozing from gummy oleoresins in the leaves' brown and papery protective sheaths, not from the leaves themselves. As they split open, for a few days we drifted through an aromatic tunnel as old as the Bible. Like birthday candles, hazel catkins trembled in fired sunlight, firing puffs of yellow pollen into bright air.

It wasn't just hot, although it certainly was, it was also refreshing. As smooth as silk, an alluring breeze fluttered through every day, teasing its way unnoticed into every cranny. Its invisible caressing fingers probed deep into places not normally warmed until July. Bumble bees hummed through glowing sheaves of daffodils. Oh! How we were all duped. Looking back, recalling the laughter and the happy surge of endorphins that wafted us through our work for the whole month, how completely we were taken in. How drugged we were by the sun's brassy overtures. I overheard someone say, 'If this is global warming, I like it. Bring it on!'

Global warming it may or may not, in the long run, prove to have been; a climatic aberration it certainly was. It was a ludicrous extreme, a ridiculous blip, a spike of perfidious deception. And we fell for it. We thought it was the early spring to crown all springs. We thought it would never end;

that it would mellifluously drowse into a summer of dreams and the bright remembered days of childhood. 'Isn't it great?' We all nodded.

⋆　　⋆　　⋆

The main road winds up the glen mimicking the meanders of the river. To the north-west the glacial valley is a wall of spiny gorse, hundreds of acres of steep, impenetrable thicket. It's one of the great delights of spring in the glen. We move in a golden dazzle of coconut and almond perfume. The gorse and broom flowers daub the sun-facing, thousand-foot slope of the valley-side in a blur of gaudy colour. Beneath it lies a dense, umber quilt of winter-killed bracken, the new crozier shoots still to appear in April. At its height in August, unshaded by trees, the bracken can reach over six feet tall. Deer vanish into its jungle in an instant. Wading through is a strength-sapping struggle against rigid, stringy stems and rough, scratchy fronds. When the frosts return in the autumn it pleases me to see it rust away, finally collapsing to a foot-snagging tangle of crinkly undergrowth, where it lies all winter. When the snows cover its tangle, it provides a haven for voles and mice, but it is also where the lissom weasel hunts unseen.

The snows were long gone. February had been dry and cold, March was now hot, and that beguiling, desiccating breeze had been insinuating its way into the dead bracken for weeks. The gorse sizzled around it, wallowing in its orgy of scent and colour. Both were as dry and crisp as cornflakes.

Longing for a beer at the end of a long hot day, my son Warwick took off for the pub three miles away. He arrived at eight thirty and at last the pint foamed in front of him. As he raised it to his lips his mobile phone rang – a friend calling from the other side of the valley. 'Sorry, mate, but do you know your house is on fire?' Warwick never got his beer.

We should have seen it coming. We were half asleep in all that sunshine. We hadn't even put out a fire warning. We all knew the bracken was tinder and the gorse was explosive. We were caught napping.

For ten minutes mobile-phone signals fizzed from the mast high above us. It was a call to arms. Some of us were in baths, others asleep; some were online, yet more slumped in front of the television after a full day's work. Glinting in the evening gloom, cars streamed, like frightened fish, the quick mile to Warwick's house. Thankfully it wasn't on fire, but the hill behind it had exploded, making it appear that the house was engulfed.

Something, perhaps a cigarette carelessly thrown from a car window, or possibly even a mindless youth 'seeing if it would burn' – something we'll never know – caused a flame to lick into that roadside bracken. In seconds it was an inferno. The breeze tunnelling down the glen quickly fanned it up the steep slope and into the dense jungle of pyrotechnically charged gorse. By the time we got there it was an unassailable wall of flame and smoke five hundred feet high, stretching a quarter of a mile down the valley towards Aigas.

Between us and the source of the fire, dotted along the

valley, are five houses. These had to be our first concern. The fire brigade, a gang of local Beauly boys, arrived with a tender and immediately radioed for more. An hour later there were eleven. They came from far and wide, their blue lights flickering through the darkness. Their screaming sirens could be seen and heard for miles before they arrived. Once we knew that the brigade boys were stationed beside each house, spraying roofs and gardens, and that the occupants were safely evacuated, we could gather our team of field staff to assess the task ahead. Young ranger trainees and old hands, all nine of us, accompanied by a tender and a professional team of firemen impressively equipped with masks and goggles, breathing apparatus, knapsack sprays and fireproof suits and helmets, progressed to the moor above the loch, to a downwind position overlooking the fire. What we saw stopped us dead in our tracks.

A mile away, a cliff of flame and smoke three hundred yards wide was surging towards us as fast as a man could run. It raged through banks of gorse and broom and was rapidly fanning out into the open heather. There was no chance of tackling it in the gorse thickets – the heat was immense – but we could at least slow its progress as it probed and zigzagged out into the heather. Hopefully we could prevent it closing in on our precious native woodlands and forestry plantations.

At this moment came a shock, which, at first, we couldn't take in. The senior officer in charge of the professional fire-crew told us that he and his men wouldn't be able to help us fight the fire. They were bound by 'health and safety regulations', he explained. After dark they were allowed only to fight fires that were threatening houses and lives. 'But it *is* heading towards us, towards our houses and our lives,' we pleaded. 'If this wind keeps up it will be on us in less than a couple of hours.'

'Sorry.' He shook his head. 'We can't help, but you can borrow our long-handled beaters.' It was no good standing arguing. With torpedoed hearts we headed towards the flames.

I can tell you that fighting a bush fire is a hell all of its own. Armed with shovels and beaters we pitched in. Warwick took charge. He lined up the team a few yards apart and attacked the vanguard of the flames charging towards us like an angry enemy. The plan was to break up the line of fire into more manageable bites.

A raging fire, a fire out of control, seems to awake some deep primeval fear within us all. For thousands of years mankind has used and abused fire in equal measure. Like water, fire is an elemental component of our lives, echoing back to our long ancestral origins; we welcome it into our homes and we would miss it terribly if we couldn't. To me a living fire is one of the essential comforts of home; as I sit and stare into the flames it seems to tug at the long leashes of our cave-dwelling past. To have to live without it would close part of me down and gnaw at my soul, denying a fragment of who I am. Yet its control is such a fine line, as anyone who has witnessed a house fire, or even a bad chimney fire, knows only too well. The sight of this blaze lighting up the night sky in a sinister orange glow, which, people told me later, could be seen fifty miles away, filled me with a deep and humbling dread.

The ranger team pitched in with vigour. Warwick, Brenna, Elspeth, Alicia, Dave, Scott, Duncan, Kate and Sarah surfed into the fray on a gut-clenching wave of adrenalin. They swung and they beat and they cursed the night air blue. They stamped and they flailed their beaters and shovels with all the gusto of rampaging Vikings. They were magnificent.

The choking smoke blackened their faces and seared their lungs. The oxygen they so desperately needed was being sucked away by the flames so that they had to turn back, coughing and spluttering to gulp cleaner air where they could find it. Their hearts thumped, like military drums, and their arms flailed endlessly, up and down, up and down, relentlessly, urgently, dangerously, often hopelessly. Their eyes, crazed with a mix of fear and tenacity, streamed tears of anguish, exhaustion and stinging pain. Still the fire came on in tireless rushes of snapping and charging flame, and always suffocating heat. No sooner had we extinguished a few yards of heather than we had to rush back because it had sprung to life again. The swirling wind dervishes, born of the sucking heat, seemed to taunt us with ever fiercer spurts of bursting, racing flame.

There was little I could do to help them. Their young arms and legs and lungs were far better suited to the fight than mine so I busied myself with ferrying water to drink and wet cloths to cool their blackened brows, stamping the embers behind them, boosting morale wherever I could. Lucy and her team of domestic helpers arrived with sandwiches, chocolate and steaming, sugary tea to fuel their energy and sloosh down their searing throats. There was no time to stop: refreshment had to be taken on the job, snatching a bite here and a swig there.

They kept going long into the night. Just when I thought they must surely collapse and give up, fired by some strange inner strength, they seemed to find a renewed burst of power to keep their flailing arms at work. It was heroic and the battle analogy was frighteningly real. Often the enemy wouldn't die. It took two, three, sometimes four blows to subdue the flame, only to find that it flared up again a few feet away to shouts of 'Look out! Behind you!' and 'Quick, it's getting away!' so that they had to turn back and flail all over again. It was as if they were fighting for their lives, calling up feats of endurance way beyond any prior assessment I could have wildly guessed at. As I stood back and watched them, a line of shadowy figures lit like entranced fire-dancing tribesmen in the smoky darkness, I felt an overwhelming wave of pride.

They kept it up all night, holding the fire at bay. Only as the dawn emerged in a steely line behind us did the brigade boys come up and join us with their smart equipment. The knapsack sprayers were a great help and I was glad to call the rangers in, back to our little environmental centre, the Magnus House, where we had set up a command post, a place to eat and wipe charred faces and collapse into a chair after many hours of punishing toil.

We had done well. Winning? Perhaps not, but we had certainly slowed the fire's progress and contained it throughout the night. Without their effort it would have reached our woodlands for sure. Elspeth, the nimblest and fittest hill runner in our team, offered to sprint up the half-mile of open moorland to Bad à Chamlain, the trig point on the high peak of the moor, to view the extent of the damage and the direction of the flames. The news she radioed in was deeply depressing. The fight was far from over and a new fire from further up the valley was now heading our way again on a brisk breeze.

What was clear was that we needed superhuman help. I asked the brigade chief to telephone for a helicopter. 'We'll be there in half an hour,' promised the control room. Helicopter fire-fighting protocols are well rehearsed in the Highlands and I knew what a boon it would be to have airborne support. The aircraft dangles a nylon bag on a long line, dunking it into a loch or river, scooping up a ton of water at a time, then flies straight to the line of flame, laying out the water in a drenching rain just where the fire would like to go.

We were lucky. The pilot was an ace. Each ton of water came at four-and-a-half-minute intervals, streaming back and forwards between the loch and the fire, the pinewoods between them thudding and swaying with the power of the blades and the downdraught. Neighbours streamed in to help at both ends of the fire. Farmers, crofters, keepers and stalkers willingly piled in, a gang of local men and boys to join the line down in the valley with the pros. Our ranger team had had an hour off, an hour of food and rest, while we took stock in the rising light of the morning.

As I looked from face to face, the young people with whom I work every day were scarcely recognisable. The smoke-blackened faces and blistered hands, the broken fingernails, the singed eyebrows, eyes rubbed red and streaming, hair in wild tangles, girls' soft complexions smudged and blotched, the boys' unshaven, charred and streaked, like commandos after a jungle skirmish.

When the helicopter thudded into view to tackle the moor, the team leaped to their feet and headed off up the hill once more. They joined the line of pros, now fifteen of us, all fighting the moorland together, Warwick directing the helicopter to douse the new fronts. I was speechless with admiration, a heart overflowing with the gratitude of a people being delivered from a vicious and brutal occupation. I stood a little way off and watched. We were winning at last.

★     ★     ★

It was to be another full day before we could be confident the dragon was dead. The brigade boys stayed with us to the bitter end, then another night just to make sure it didn't spring to life again. The ordeal was over. We had lost about two hundred acres of scrub and another hundred of moorland, all consumed in Shakespeare's 'violent ends'. Twenty-four hours later it rained – the first wet day for six weeks – and as April arrived it snowed.

We had crashed from the sublime to the absurd and alarming. Winter returned not just to Scotland but right across the UK, with swirling rage and dramatic destruction.

On 3 April the *Telegraph* reported:

> Tens of thousands of homes have been affected by power cuts over the last two days, as companies blamed snow for the disruption. Motorways were jammed as perilous ice and frozen snow forced drivers to slow down, with drifts up to seven feet high on exposed higher ground. Yesterday, a snow plough – sent out to rescue a stranded motorist – came off the road itself and had to be rescued by gritters, while unsuspecting campers woke up to waist-high snow on the North Yorkshire moors.

Temperatures plummeted. Here at Aigas we recorded –8° Celsius overnight on 4 April. Sharp frost continued for a full week. This was much more than old Dunc Macrae's lambing storm. It was just the sort of extreme climatic aberration we had been warned would characterise climate change. It was sudden and severe, actually the worst April weather for thirty years. Even when temperatures began to lift, brooding clouds dominated our days. Rain and wind kept our heads down and our collars up. April would eventually record 250 per cent of normal rainfall for the Moray Firth area.

The fire had been a huge distraction at the end of our heatwave, and it continued to be so as we tried to assess the damage it might have done to wildlife, particularly to ground-nesting birds and, doubtless, invertebrates too, although mercifully the nesting season was barely under way. It would be many more weeks before we could draw any firm conclusions. Now, looking back, we know that, frightening and potentially disastrous though the fire was, it was but a missed note in the bigger opera of that unseasonable heat wave and its abrupt reversal into winter, followed by the soggiest spring for years. None of us had any idea how devastating it would be to so much around us – but that comes later.

## 13

# Buzzard

High, high, buzzard, high
From scarce moving wings
Suspended in the sky
Tear, tear your metallic scream
From the lava lungs
Molten through the throat.
Terror, terror is struck,
Into the soft gloved ear;
And the frantic brain
Spins the limbs to action,
Or to frozen fear –
Of the butchering plummet,
      the entering claw,
Of the sweeping sickle,
And the ravening maw.

'Buzzard', J.L-K.

April normally means buzzard. Wings suspended in the sky, circling high. It is now that they pair off and display, often two or three pairs together in a spiral of reaching pinions, turning, tilting, wings and backs glinting in the bright sunlight between bursts of fizzing showers. I hear their

189

blade-thin cries slicing the new day soon after sunrise. A glance upward tells me that again this year they will nest in the birch wood behind the loch.

Few birds and sounds so roundly augment this landscape. We have golden eagles and ospreys and peregrines, all iconic species of the wild Highlands, of course, but I see those species as the lofty aristocrats who may or may not deign to grace us with their presence, the occasional ormolu on the satinwood frame of our glens and hills. But buzzards are the yeomen of everyday occurrence, the working tenantry of the land, and a buttress to the fabric of our days. As the robins and rooks are to the gardens, so the buzzards are to the fields and woods and moors. They are a given, expected and required. Our woods would not be the same without them.

As a small boy of perhaps seven or eight, I was walking through an English wood with my father. We came to a clearing where pheasants had been fed grain from a hopper. There, in a tangle of pale feathers, lay a dead buzzard, recently shot or poisoned by a gamekeeper. I had never seen a buzzard close up before. In fact, even if one had been pointed out to me as a silhouette in the sky, I don't think I had ever properly imagined what it was like. Now it was here, at my feet. My father wouldn't let me touch it for fear that it was contaminated with strychnine, the poison regularly used back then, but gingerly he held it up by a primary feather and its broad outstretched wings dangled four feet to the ground. The silence and the charged pathos of the moment are as vivid to me now as if it were yesterday.

In those days buzzards were an uncommon sight in the countryside throughout Britain. They had been persecuted – shot on sight, trapped and poisoned for killing pheasant poults and partridges – to such an extent that they had been driven out of the farmed countryside and survived only in remote and mountainous regions. They are still persecuted in some places today, but the protection afforded them by the 1981 Wildlife and Countryside Act has enabled a steady recovery to their present status of being possibly the commonest bird of prey in Britain, at around 80,000 pairs. They are also highly visible. Their habit of perching on telegraph poles and other prominent viewing points, their soaring spirals on bright days of lifting thermals and their mewing cry (much abused in television dramas the moment a scene goes anywhere near a forest, a mountain or a moor), all blend to make the buzzard's presence very obvious.

> Two buzzards,
> Still-wings, each
> Magnetised to the other,
> Float orbits.
>
> 'March Morning Unlike Others',
> Ted Hughes

So successful has their recovery been that there is now talk from sporting lobby groups of lifting legal protection or even 'a licensed cull' of buzzards in and around pheasant shoots, an action that could be technically possible under the terms of the Act, as it is with fish-eating goosanders and cormorants on salmon rivers. There is no doubt that buzzards kill pheasant poults. It is hardly surprising that if thousands of young, inexperienced game birds are released together in one place they are going to create a honey pot of attraction for predators of all sorts. I have some sympathy for gamekeepers who do their best to guard against predation by carefully siting their feeders and release pens and by providing lots of cover for the young pheasants, but I would never support lifting the legal protection for birds of prey and certainly not 'a cull' of any kind.

We have seen only too clearly what happens when there is no legal protection for wildlife. We have lived through dismal eras of not just persecution but of annihilation of our native wildlife in the name of game shooting and direct and indirect commercial exploitation. I have no reason to believe that the same thing wouldn't happen again. For me it boils down to a matter of ethics, of personal philosophy and national responsibility.

Man's record of looking after wildlife is grim. A free-for-all for whales for commercial gain in the eighteenth and nineteenth centuries drove several species to the very brink of extinction. We still have to argue fiercely at the International Whaling Commission to prevent that happening again. Penguins used to be rendered down for their blubber and seal pups were skinned alive for their fur. In Canada by 1877 tundra swans had been hunted for their quill feathers down to the last sixty-nine birds left in the wild. Beavers were hunted to extinction for their fur throughout a dozen European countries. Elephants were and still are slaughtered for their ivory, and the Chinese market for rhinoceros horn remains a threat to the survival of critically endangered African rhinos. The list goes on and on.

In a country of starving people, it is very hard to argue that wildlife should come before people – impossible to say, to an African hunter, 'You can't feed your family today,' because the bird or antelope he wants to kill is endangered. But in a wealthy country like Britain there can be no valid argument against protecting wildlife, with measures in place to mitigate against serious pests to food production and injurious or disease-carrying species, such as rats.

Economic arguments, such as those wheeled out by the game-shooting fraternity – 'This estate needs commercial pheasant shooting to survive' – aren't really economic arguments at all. They are code for 'We want to shoot pheasants or grouse or partridges and we don't want wildlife to interfere with that.' To argue their case at an economic level is to imply that the estate has no choice, whereas, of course, there are many ways in which estates can and do make money without having to engage in commercial shooting. There are also many ways of conducting a shoot and of developing a sporting culture that works with wildlife rather than against it.

I entirely accept that it may not be possible to shoot as *many* pheasants, partridges or grouse by doing things differently, but I seriously question whether the enjoyment of shooting necessarily requires a huge bag. Some of the very best shooting days I have ever had have been what are called 'rough' days of walking with a gundog and two or three friends; days when we have taken healthy exercise, tested our skills and accuracy, thoroughly enjoyed the fresh air and ended the day with a mixed bag of pigeons, a few pheasants, a brace of partridges, a couple of rabbits and a hare, perhaps even a duck or a goose. For me those memorable shooting days are enhanced by seeing a buzzard and a red kite, perhaps a peregrine or a hen harrier, occasions when we can stop and admire their aerobatic agility and delight in the diversity of our countryside.

I'm not arguing against responsible shooting. I was reared in the country among shooting and hunting people; I was very predatory in my youth, shooting most species on the quarry list from ptarmigan on the snowy mountain tops to standing up to my waist in the freezing slush of a tidal ditch on a January dawn waiting for a flight of wild geese. Before the myxomatosis virus decimated rabbits in Britain in the 1960s, and when they were a serious agricultural pest, I remember shooting rabbits at harvest time until the barrels of my gun were so hot that I couldn't hold them. Game shooting is an important recreation and social activity in the countryside, but it sometimes gets out of control.

In the past Britain's shooting culture has operated strong ethical standards and codes of practice, but those have slowly eroded as the sport has been commercialised as a result of sharp changes in leisure time and the availability of the sport at every level in society. At the same time agriculture has been industrialised, hedges ripped out and fields purged of invertebrate 'pests' and 'weeds', so that the opportunities for wild game species, notably the native grey partridge and

feral pheasants, to survive and breed in the wild have radi-
cally reduced, thereby necessitating that shoots buy in reared
birds for release.

Often in pretty unsavoury battery conditions the game-
farm industry now produces some thirty-five million
pheasant poults for release into the British countryside every
year. I recently learned with horror of one English estate
that 'put down' (a euphemism for 'released into fields and
woods') 150,000 reared pheasants, partridges and mallard
ducks every year so that a continuous procession of commercial shooters could be flown in for a day's massacre of birds
forced into the air by battalions of beaters, six days a week
throughout the shooting season. I was told that a digger had
dug a mass grave in the form of a long trench so that the
virtually valueless shot birds could be tipped in and buried.

Practices such as these are not sport; nor are they ethical.
They are a disgrace and will eventually bring the whole
shooting world into disrepute. The authorities and game
lobby groups need to act quickly to outlaw such gross
infringements of what should be a reputable and responsible
country activity. I cannot help observing that many of those
pheasants, whether as poults just released, killed on roads
or wounded with shot and crawling off to die, will have
been substantially responsible for fuelling the sharp rise in
buzzard numbers throughout the UK. No, for me, along
with other birds of prey, the buzzard remains an enjoyable
signal of countryside diversity, not a threat to be vilified and
'controlled'. And what would come next? Herons at fish
farms? Ospreys on fishing rivers and streams? Peregrines on

grouse moors? Golden eagles? Why not control otters that have the temerity to eat fish?

Before leaving this subject there is one more angle to explore – actually a much more far-reaching and urgent aspect of the countryside-management debate and one already alluded to. Those memorable days of rough shooting almost always took place on old-style farmland where there was a broad mix of long-established habitats. There would be rough pasture for sheep and cattle, arable cropland of plough or stubble, root and cover crops, all broken up by windbreak copses of tight-packed conifers, dense hedgerows, old stone walls, boggy and marshy corners of fields, stagnant ponds, patches of scrubland, thickets of hawthorn, broom and gorse, gentle woods of native trees of all ages and many different species. This uplifting mosaic of habitats would always be bound to produce some rabbits and a hare or two, a covey of partridges and a few pheasants, one or two mallard and plenty of wood pigeons. It is also a sound descriptor of Countryside, with a capital C. It is what Countryside perhaps could be like again, at least in some areas. Add to this cock-tail some open heather moorland, windswept mountains and lakes, a bog or a fen, and you have achieved a nature-conservation ideal rich in wildlife. But that is not the reality of the world we live in.

What we have is 78 per cent of the UK landmass locked into industrialised agri-business of cropland mechanically and chemically purged of everything that lives and moves except the desired crop. Perhaps as much as 80 per cent of farmland in our countryside is dominated by these agricultural monocultures dedicated to food production. We should not be surprised that shoots have to import reared pheasants.

In recent years, farmers, conservationists and governments have worked much more closely to re-create threatened habitats and to move towards a richer biodiversity. There are many commendable 'stewardship', 'wider countryside' and 'native woodland' schemes, and there are many farmers, big and small, who really believe in maintaining a healthy diversity of wildlife on their farms. European funds are paying for hedges to be planted again. There is also a slowly expanding organic sector, but the reality remains that the huge majority of cropland has to be fed with fertilisers, sprayed with pesticides and prepared and harvested with giant machines.

Livestock farms are mechanised too. Single-species leys of nutritious rye grass have replaced ancient flower- and clover-rich pastures; meadows have vanished, and cattle and sheep are dosed with systemic drugs to eliminate pests and diseases, often resulting in toxic dung, which, instead of being a vital food source for invertebrates, kills off bugs, beetles and flies in the fields. That is the world we live in and the dog-and-stick days of buttercup-twirling yore are not likely to return anytime soon.

Worthy though many of these schemes are, we have been very slow to understand that we face an invertebrate crisis in Britain. The knock-on effect of decades of chemical farming (fertilisers are chemicals) is that the most basic foundation of biodiversity, the microbes in the soil and the invertebrates – bugs, beetles, bees, butterflies and other beasties most of us have never heard of – all of which serve to feed most birds and ultimately just about everything else, have been slowly and silently declining; the seed-bearing weeds upon which so many invertebrates and birds depend have been selectively poisoned out. Stewardship schemes unquestionably help, but until we face up to the looming invertebrate crisis and begin to restore these essential building blocks of wildlife habitats, vast swathes of our countryside will remain locked in sterile paralysis.

It is sad that conflicts between farming, shooting and nature conservation tend to be polarised. I have enjoyed shooting and been a livestock farmer on a modest scale for forty years. I am very well versed in the economic arguments, but I also care passionately about wildlife. Working with nature rather than directly against it is always likely to be more successful for everyone – a principle we are often slow to acknowledge. It was those two soaring buzzards this morning that brought me back to my desk and I am grateful to them for that.

*    *    *

After beginning with a snowstorm, April descended into a washout. It rained and rained. Winds racked the trees and the land was sodden. One morning I awoke to an uncanny silence. The recent and entirely normal racket of the rooks was gone. I went to the window and stared out at the rain-filled skies. I couldn't see a single black silhouette in the rookery trees. Hurriedly I dressed and took the dogs out, walking briskly the hundred and fifty yards to the first nests. Silence.

I knew they had laid eggs early in March because husks of hatched shells appeared on the twig-strewn and guano-spattered grass beneath the trees. The incubating parent birds had hunkered down inside the nest cups, invisible from the ground, but as the temperature hovered around freezing and snow squalls came barrelling through, I had a sinking feeling that they were fighting a losing battle.

I had also watched them at work in the fields, searching for food, where they strode about in rowdy gangs and seemed to be finding something to eat, probing here and there, plunging their sharp, four-inch bills into the soggy turf. Then came the frost: –8° Celsius for a week. Bright sun by day, swingeing cold by night. The full moon fell on 6 April. With it came an anticyclone that sucked any remaining heat from the land. Overnight the temperature plunged to –12° Celsius. Everything froze.

The rooks were in turmoil. Feeding in the frozen fields became hopeless and, anyway, any emerging bugs would have been killed off. For several days hungry rooks flew round their rookery trees cawing loudly. They had pitched on the nests and taken off again straight away, seeming to signal that they had no food for the delicate young chicks.

The chicks should now have been well on and constantly crying for food. There should have been a cacophony of rook gossip, to-ing and fro-ing of parent birds, and the gargling burble of strong chicks calling as their gaping mouths were stuffed with regurgitated food. Instead, the leaden silence of emptiness. Nothing moved. Not a single rook was in attendance at this crucial moment in their breeding calendar. Quite simply, they had given up and gone. Twenty-nine nests, and possibly as many as a hundred chicks, abandoned. They had all starved.

I don't know where they went, but it seems likely that they had joined up with other rooks on the east coast where there was less frost and where the arable soils delivered up a more reliable supply of food. I was gutted. In forty years of living at Aigas I had never known the rookery fail. We missed their baggy-legged bustling, their bossing and bullying and their constant corvid backchat. My morning baths had lost their appeal. The dawns were strangely silent and the skies disturbingly empty. They had given up and gone from our lives.

A few days later, still lamenting the loss of our rooks as I walked the Jack Russells early one morning, a movement among the nests caught my eye. I looked up to see two black birds. My heart leaped. Perhaps, after all, at least one rook nest had survived. I moved to a better place and homed in with binoculars. My spirits tumbled into a downward somersault of macabre confirmation. They weren't rooks: they were carrion crows feeding off the dead chicks in the rooks' nests. Corvid eating corvid. Rook chicks die: crow chicks thrive. Nature isn't choosy; it just gets on with it. It's an ill wind that blows nobody any good.

★   ★   ★

I began to realise what had happened. March had been glorious. All that warmth had brought with it an exceptionally early Highland spring. Buds had unfurled, chloroplasts had streamed, and deep in the secret crannies of the soil invertebrate larvae, especially leatherjackets, had awoken from long sleep and wiggled to within three inches of the surface, later to emerge as crane flies. The rooks had loved it. Every day I had seen them out there, gorging on these fat, protein-filled delicacies. Right across the landscape life had awoken exceptionally early. The benison of solar energy and heat had created a false dawn of fecundity. Everyone was fooled. Then came the snow and the swingeing frosts. A week of −8° Celsius will always be a killer of young and tender life. A whole age class of invertebrates was wiped out before it had got going. There were no leatherjackets left, no bugs to feed the rook chicks.

When, later in April, the swallows and house martins arrived back from Africa, there were no flying insects to feed them. They went away again. The great tits, an irrepressible species if ever there was one, abandoned their nests of young. One pair that had previously nested successfully in a box fitted with a camera under the eaves of our environmental education centre did manage to lay a single egg and raise one chick – that from a species capable of laying a clutch of six to ten eggs and raising them all. There were no caterpillars to feed the adults or the young. Just about everything had been deceived, lulled into false security by the errant sun, then massacred like innocents by the sudden return of winter.

# 14

# Comings and Goings

What I cannot see, no matter how closely I look, is what drives this small creature, barely heavier than air, to make the journeys that it must make. What thousands of miles have passed beneath its stubby wings, which seem so ill-suited to the task but which have carried it back here again. It knows and I do not.

*Living on the Wind*, Scott Weidensaul

The world's favorite season is the spring.
All things seem possible in May.
*Circle of the Seasons*, Edwin Way Teale

Somehow we arrived at May, but you would have been forgiven for not knowing it. April had plunged us back into winter; the buds and leaves that had so exuberantly burst in March were now frost-scorched and shrivelled. Day after day an icy rain spat upon Scotland, now sleet, now flurrying snow that shrouded our dawns, making us think that March and April had been a turbulent dream and that we were really still stuck in February.

A north-east wind kept us well wrapped throughout April; to venture out was to reach instinctively for a hat, gloves and a scarf. No thought of shedding a garment of any kind for the first eleven days of May. May! Where were your darling buds and surging hormones? We were bewildered; the birds were befuddled; the bugs were nowhere to be seen. Yet despite everything, a tentative greening did creep back into our world. Surreptitiously, uncertainly, almost suspiciously, ought-not-to-be-here-like -- the trees leafed up again.

Then, with ill-concealed relief, the tune of the television weather reporters changed. They turned prophet with a smile. Off the map to the east, approaching Scandinavia from eastern Europe they had spotted a large high-pressure zone expanding, sliding sideways and outwards towards us, like ripples on a pond that grew and grew. Windless in its tranquil core, and very stealthily, it spread its heartening gospel to the west until it embraced most of northern Europe.

The bookies nervously halved their odds for a record-breaking May temperature from 16:1 to 8:1. Overnight on 21 May it arrived. The clouds vanished. By morning our temperature had rocketed from the unseasonal chill of 9° Celsius to 24°. By midday at Altnaharra in Sutherland, an hour and a half's drive to the north of us, the temperature zoomed to 27.3° Celsius – just 1.7° short of an all-time record for May. No wonder the bookies were twitchy. What they had boasted as a safe bet had become a real possibility in just thirty-six hours. As the temperatures levelled off, their sigh of relief was audible.

We'd had the wettest April for a century and the coldest for twenty-three years. Now May was heading for the record books too. A headline in the *Daily Mail* trumpeted that Inverness, only sixteen miles to our east, was hotter than

Ibiza. With withering *sangfroid*, Mike Silverstone, head of the BBC's weather centre, observed, 'May can be a very fickle month. Weather in spring can be very varied.'

The thing about heat and sun is that it pumps up the endorphins; everyone smiles. When you're smiling you tend not to notice the downside. Of course, we loved it. Just as we had back in March, we swanned about in T-shirts and no shirts, in sandals and shorts, sun hats and shades. We fell into the loch, even though the dark, peaty water was barely 9° Celsius. And, just as it had in March, it took our breath away. We didn't care: we had waited weeks for this.

In the first few days of that surge of endorphins, as I sat in a deck-chair beside the loch one balmy afternoon, faint strains of the unmistakable, squeaky-scratchy chatter of wild geese came to my ears. Looking up, shading my squinting eyes, I could just make out a broad skein high above me in a long, wavering V. They were greylags, flying at four or five thousand feet, fifty or sixty of them, strung out in constantly shifting formation, like performing jets. These were not local, non-migratory greylags just drifting about Scotland, they were migrating – of that I am sure. They were heading north, back to their breeding grounds in Iceland nearly a month later than normal, going home. They must have been the straggling last few; for whatever reason, they had lingered. Perhaps the winds had been wrong; perhaps the roller-coaster weather had confused them too. Perhaps they had wintered in the Low Countries and had taken a detour, dawdled across to us to try to find a favourable wind to carry them back to nest in the tundra wastes of Iceland, now just emerging from eight months of winter.

Were they adapting, responding to climate change before my very eyes? Was I witnessing a shift in behaviour by these robust, archetypal geese, which for decades have been successfully expanding their numbers and their range right across northern Europe?

Some farmers don't like geese stealing their grass and winter corn, but it is our own fault. On the back of modern agriculture we have supplied them with just what they need: potato and stubble fields when they arrive for winter, keeping them fat with winter-sown cereals, the stronger and fitter for the migration home in spring, the more likely to breed successfully. Can geese choose their migration dates at will? I don't know the answers to these questions, but I do know that geese and swans (and probably many other birds) have to learn their migration routes.

The work of Canadian ornithologist H. Albert Hochbaum, published in 1955 from many years' study at the Delta Waterfowl Research Station in Manitoba, demonstrated that goose migration – in his case Canada goose migration – is a learned behaviour passed down from parent to offspring. Subsequent studies on other geese have demonstrated that his findings stand for most migratory species of *Anatidae* – the goose family – in the northern hemisphere. He suggests that the approximate timing of migration is innate, triggered by length of daylight hours, as are the orientation and celestial navigation skills present in most birds, but that in geese these can be and are superseded by direct learning and experience. Female geese are hard-wired to return to their birthplace every spring, but not the males. The pairs bond and the males just tag along, back to their self-evidently successful nesting grounds. Come the autumn, when it's time to head south again as the frosts descend and the Arctic winter closes in, the young birds are led south by their parents in tightly knit family groups, learning the route, the stop-overs, the feeding grounds and the best places to over-winter. Hochbaum called this learned behaviour 'traditions'. If they can learn all that, I feel sure they can learn to adjust those traditions to allow for freaky weather too.

★   ★   ★

Back in the blowsy but short-lived treachery of March's heat wave, the first swallows and house martins had arrived in Scotland. They had been sighted over Loch Ness, only a few minutes' skimming flight away. But they hadn't come to us. I was glad. It was too early, and I knew from bitter experience that those early birds find nothing to eat and are forced to go away again, back to lower, more sheltered landscapes or to the coast, where they can flick along the beaches for sand flies. In the slicing chill of April one or two birds had arrived in the glen, but they were gone again straight away. But hardy wheatears had arrived on the moors, and the first brave willow warblers had been heard cascading defiantly from the birch woods.

Now, in mid-May, with all this bursting warmth, the full rush of summer migrants piled in, almost as though they had been queuing just down the road, like impatient shoppers waiting for opening time. Cuckoos prattled and cuck'd from the hill behind the loch, and tree pipits were suddenly spilling their shrill whistles and trills from the bright lime-budded tips of larches. Chiffchaffs announced themselves from the willows at the marsh and whitethroats chittered from those banks of golden broom and gorse left after the fire. Warwick opened his front door to find an exhausted redstart on the mat. He brought it to work to show me – we don't get many here: we haven't got enough of their favoured habitat of mature oaks. After a rest it seemed to perk up and fluttered up into a sycamore. Now at least there were a few insects about to boost its strength.

For me the real joy of that warmth was the return of our blackcaps. They, too, were almost a month late, but they came. The dawns, now at three forty-five a.m., pulsing towards the summer solstice at eight minutes of increased daylight every day, rang with their fluting, melodic exuberance. There is a large clump of snowberry in the garden much loved by both wrens and blackcaps. Brambles entwine its woody stems, making it impenetrable even to my probing inquisitions. I peer into nothing but twiggy darkness. But I suspect it is a haven for spiders and consequently for anything that enjoys a spider repast. I can rely upon that shrubbery for the first blackcaps of the year and it hasn't let me down yet. Later on, when they start to nest they move much more freely through the gardens and trees so that all day our little world floats aloft, enriched by the sheer joy of their constantly repeating canticle.

I read that in southern England blackcaps are now present all the year round. It seems that the warming climate and food, particularly fat balls, on suburban bird tables has meant that they can survive. But these are thought not to be our migratory birds, but another 'new' strain of central European and Scandinavian blackcaps that have started to migrate away from Continental cold to the much milder winters of England's south and south-west – a shorter migration, a better climate and a more reliable source of food. That's how adaptation works: life keeps moving on.

I can't be sure where our blackcaps go in winter, but I read that it's southern Europe, the Mediterranean countries and further even to sub-Saharan Africa. I find it hard to comprehend that the little scrap of ashen feathers I held in my hand last autumn had made it all that way and back again, possibly several times. Like Scott Weidensaul, I am dazzled. That tiny pulsing heart, those fluttering wings, the beady eyes scanning the land beneath, and that fizzing brain no bigger than my little fingernail, all perfectly in sync, like a tiny electric toy. All driving, pushing, steering, navigating, eyeing up the stars, sharp little bill thrust into the wind, skimming across seas, weaving through woods, fields, gardens and parks, orchards, vineyards and olive groves, flickering over mountains and dales, skirting great lakes and snatching a roost and a rest wherever strength and energy supplies demand. Is it two thousand miles, or three? Does it take a week or two, or three, even a month? I don't know, and until some boffin manages to radio tag or track a black-cap's migration, I don't suppose anyone else can be sure either. But it doesn't matter. What matters to me is that it makes it there and back again safely. I would rejoice if I could find a way to tell it how very pleased I am.

$$\star \qquad \star \qquad \star$$

It was only then, still basking in the warmth of what would turn out to be a disappointingly brief spring, the memory of which is made the more piquant by the sorrowful summer that would follow, that I realised the full extent of the damage that treacherous burst of heat in March had done. All those life forms that had been tricked, lured into exposing themselves far too early, had been ruthlessly obliterated by the subsequent frosts and snows, many never to emerge again. The buds and blossoms that had flung themselves apart; the tender leaves that had sloughed off their protective sheaths; the bugs, the beetles, the butterflies and moths that had crawled out of hibernation or pupae that had split; larvae that had prematurely rushed their next instar phase; frogs and toads that had pumped their spawn into pools that would soon be smothered by an inch of ice; birds, such as the rooks, that had laid their eggs and hatched their chicks into a world of frost and starvation. Everything had suffered. If it was a roller-coaster for us, it was a death slide for them.

$$\star \qquad \star \qquad \star$$

Climate change. I am wary of that catch-all excuse for anything we can't explain or don't like. Its brackets are too large, too all-embracing – a tad too convenient. The rub that leaves me uncomfortably pensive is that we simply don't know. What little I do know tells me that, however real climate change is, it is unlikely to be the sole reason for those changes to the natural world we can see and document. It is when several factors come together, bringing an insupportable pressure to bear upon species and ecosystems, that things go most seriously wrong.

Perhaps this is what we have to expect now: massive swings and surges; unreliable seasons; soaring and plunging temperatures; exceptional storms and their consequent floods. Have we done this? Have we brought it on ourselves? Are the excesses of the Industrial Revolution to blame? How much worse will it get? Is this to be Gaia's nemesis? The scientists continue to argue and no one really knows what is happening and how it will alter our lives. But the rooks know, and the great tits and the crane flies and the looping caterpillars. They all know that they have to adapt quickly if they are to survive.

Have we got it all wrong? Has the march of what we have labelled 'civilisation' now taken us so far away from nature, from biorhythms, from contact with the soil that we have lost the ability to assess what damage our actions inflict upon the planet? Have we abandoned the precautionary principle, or did it never really exist? Does it remain simply a notion, two catchy words that never stood a chance against the march of our irrepressible greed? Or then again, was all this destined to happen anyway? Has one major event on the surface of the sun spun us into disarray, just as has almost

certainly happened many times before during the four thousand million years of life on Earth?

That certainly was the well-aired view of the former
Astronomer Royal, the late Sir Bernard Lovell FRS, who told
me shortly before he died that the fuss we were making
about climate change was 'laughable' in the context of the
planet's history. He was a man who knew a thing or two
about the sun and the Milankovitch cycle and solar flares,
about axial tilt and the precession index, all those tricks on
our eccentric path around the sun which dictate the levels
of solar radiation on Earth and are supposed to ordain the
measure of our seasons. It's hard to shrug off the opinion
of such a venerable old scientist, especially one who, at the
very end of his long life, was busy planting an oak wood
for future generations. 'It's the best thing I can do for the
planet,' he said, with a wry smile. 'Don't stand about. Come
and help me.'

At Aigas we have gone green – actually been heading
green for decades. We do respect the precautionary principle,
and if there is something sensible we can do, whether it
works or not, we're prepared to give it a fair wind. We have
reduced our carbon footprint where we can. We've installed
biomass-boilers and ground-source heat pumps, photo-
voltaic panels and solar collectors; we've composted our
waste and insulated our houses, and we have preached
sustainability to the thousands of school pupils who come
through our environmental education programmes, but we
have done so on a wing and a prayer. Our environmental
education centre, the Magnus House, is even a

demonstration of sustainable building techniques. We capped the source of building materials at fifty miles, using only locally grown timber, and we used no nasty chemicals in the building at all in order to create a hypo-allergenic environment for school-kids. The insulation is plastic water bottles shredded and spun into an inert wool, applied thirteen inches thick to walls and ceilings. The roof is turf from the neighbouring field, lifted and laid by hand.

We can measure exactly how much energy we are consuming and precisely how much electricity or fuel oil we save by these actions, but we have no way of knowing whether it will make any difference. Our principle has been: 'If it seems like a good idea and is likely to reduce man's impact, let's try it.' Like Sir Bernard, we know that our efforts are not likely to benefit us very much in our time, but perhaps for those who come after us . . . Who knows?

# 15

# Nesting

Her black pebble-eyes dazed
With waiting, the mother snaps
Alive at my presence, grabs
Air, screaming – reveals her shining
Hoard: luminous with heat,
Four freckled ovals of perfect
Sky . . .

'The Thrush's Nest', Richard Ryan

Where clumps of bramble berries are
The haychat makes her slighty bed
Dead airiff stalks and horses hair
And glues or sewed with spiders thread
And many are the spots indeed
She tries . . .

'Birds Nest III (The Haychat)', John Clare

I still don't know what made me look. I was out walking
– just being out because the May sun was smiling and the
sky I could see from my window shone like polished lapis
lazuli, as beckoning blue as the tiny petals of milkwort now
blooming on the moor. I'd been stuck at my desk for hours

and I badly needed to get out. So I wasn't looking for
anything, nor was I really thinking about much. I was saun-
tering, dawdling, idling along, gulping down the warm afternoon air, heading nowhere in particular. The orchard grass
was thick with fresh growth, dragging on my feet, and bright
with the year's first buttercups and wood anemones. I
suppose I must have been looking down, brain in the clouds,
but feet instinctively avoiding the clumps of naturalised
daffodils now rapidly dying back.

Can it be that after years of training your eyes they merge
with instinct? Can they meld into that fabled sixth sense we
so often speak about? A dry-stone diker once told me that
when looking at a pile of stones he knew instinctively which
one would best fit the gap he needed to fill. 'Instinct?' I
quizzed, as diplomatically as I could. 'Experience, surely.'

'All right,' he said, laughing, 'it's both. Let's call it intuition.'

So perhaps it was intuition. I should have a trained eye
by now: I've been searching for birds' nests for more than
fifty years. But I certainly wasn't searching that afternoon,
not thinking bird at that moment, even more certainly not
willow warbler. The last willow warbler's nest I'd found a
year ago was low down in the wisteria creeper on the
garages, a tiny grassy-licheny-feathery cup securely wedged
between the woody stem of the vine and the wall. She sat
so tight that I could gently part the leaves and peek straight
in.

But that afternoon something stopped me on my gentle
amble through the orchard's withering daffodil spears and

brown-tissued blooms. We don't cut the grass until the daffs' leaves have browned off altogether, keen to get every last pulse of solar energy into the bulbs to shore them up for their long, subterranean wait, so the grasses around them – timothy, cocksfoot and Yorkshire fog – surge upward in rampant competition with each other for the new, fresh sun. I must have been glancing down.

I stopped. There, not six feet in front of me, was an eye. Just one, a tiny black bead, fixed and shining through a slender gap in the grass stems. I froze, and I knew with that same time-honed instinct that it was a bird. I was staring into the jet fovea of a small bird's eye. I stepped back, slowly, then again and again. I stood still. The eye still stared, unblinking, as rigid as a gem set in stone. Gently and slowly I raised my binoculars. The bead had a fawn stripe running through it and a hint of lemon beneath. That was all I could see.

A willow warbler (*Phylloscopus trochilus* – the cascading leaf-watcher) is an unexceptional little bird, often our first summer migrant, an arrival announced by the male birds rendering a rippling, descending peal of pure notes tinged with mild complaint, but as pretty as a summer waterfall. It's a refrain that rings through the spring woods, repeating over and over again, lifting to a brief, pleading crescendo, then slowing as it falls and, *diminuendo*, fades away at the end. It seems to be calling out, 'Now that I've arrived, what am I going to do?'

I can bring myself to forgive those who would write it off as a little brown bird. It is famously difficult to watch, even with binoculars, because it favours leafy trees and never sits still as it flits from branch to twig, searching for spiders, aphids, caterpillars and leaf bugs. And I freely admit that it's not the most exciting bird to see. But when at last you do get a proper view its other qualities emerge and you find it isn't brown at all. Across its head, back and wings it is the late-summer green of fading willow leaves with the palest grapefruit-yellow throat and underbelly. It has a sharp little bill, straight and to the point, perfect for snatching bugs.

Like the blackcap, it resides in that large family of typical warblers that come and go every summer without any fuss, unnoticed except by ornithologs like me and a few thousand binocular-toting others to whom these tiny creatures assume an importance far greater than their size. If they've heard of a willow warbler at all, the vast generality of people don't know that it has just completed a global marathon, back from wintering in southern Africa, a migration of three thousand miles of skimming arid plains, dodging desert sandstorms and leap-frogging seas and mountains, and they probably wouldn't care much either. 'All little brown birds are the same to me,' I'm told, over and over again. But not to me: for me they all carry meaning and I thirst to know more.

*Sylviidae*, the family that used to be called the Old World Warblers and are now just Leaf Warblers, is a huge group with hundreds of species world-wide, although taxonomist boffins have rendered them into many different genera, a process now thrown into glorious confusion by the arrival of DNA testing, none of which bothers the willow warbler one jot. They are insectivorous and they favour deciduous woodland clearings, of which birch and willow seem to be among the most alluring. It is by far our commonest warbler at Aigas. Years ago they used to be called willow wrens, although they certainly aren't wrens. I remember my good friend the late Julian Clough – a dedicated amateur naturalist of the old school if ever there was one and a staunch recorder for the Scottish Ornithologists' Club – telling me that his local woods were 'lousy with willow wrens'! He was right. In May and June our birch woods resound with ever-repeating peals of their querulous, catechistic jingle.

Here am I, standing in the long grass, peering down through binoculars. There is this little bird, fixed onto its eggs in freeze mode until such time as I become too great a threat. I don't want to disturb it, so I back off to a post-and-rail fence fifteen yards away. I settle down in the sunshine and wait. It could have been a long wait, but today I am in luck. The afternoon sun was strong and the bird knew it was okay to nip off for a feed, or a wash, or perhaps just to flex her wings after a long stint of incubation.

As soon as she had left I took a look. Five tiny white eggs flecked with red pepper. The nest was crafted from woven grasses and entirely lined with feathers – feathers of all sorts – some big, some minute and fluffy. I didn't touch it, but in the curved rim of the nest I could see the speckled grey breast feathers of guinea fowl from Lucy's hen run; some were a softer grey and white from, I'm quite sure, a wood pigeon.

A few days before I had seen the carcass, a sparrowhawk

kill, plucked feathers scattered to the winds. Some other feathers were too small to tell whose they had been, perhaps even the warbler's own. The nest curved in at the top, almost creating a globe with an open top smaller than the bowl below, so that when she was on and snuggled down she was barely visible. And it was deep: the eggs nestled fully three inches below the rim, couched in a feather bed. I backed off again, quickly.

In six minutes she was back, flitting from tree to tree until she was close, then a pause, a moment of anxious hesitation because instinctively she knew that this last dip down to the nest is the one that could give her nest away to predators. Then she was down, down and shuffling round through 150 degrees until she was comfortably settled, bare brood patches on her underbelly delivering 36.6–37° Celsius of heat pulsing straight onto the eggs. Her minute leaf-like form entirely filled the opening, trapping in the heat and closing it off with the smooth, olive-fawn feathers of her back fluffed out. Her head lowered and merged with her back, hunkered down. The only hint that there was anything there at all was that tiny, ever-watching jewel of an eye.

What had made her choose that place? What was so right about it that action fired into place in her half-ounce, peanut-sized cranium? Why not here where I'm standing, where the grass and the daffs look exactly the same or, better still, securely in a thicket? Why not back in the wisteria? We can fiddle about with DNA and invent all the new genera we like, but we still know so very little when it comes to it.

I like to think it was intuition; that she, too, could blend instinct with experience and come up with a perfect fit. Perhaps she was born into a grass nest herself and the memory of flickering sunlight and the breeze-rustle of grasses was wired into her taut little brain, claiming her back to the orchard just as the salmon is drawn to its natal river to spawn. And once here the nostalgic rightness of the orchard and that particular grassy space flooded over her so powerfully that she just went for it, plucking and weaving the blades, round and round, crafting them, like clay on a potter's wheel, until the nest was a perfect circle. Then the search for the feather lining. Off to the hen run in short, darting sallies, dipping down to snatch them, one at a time, instinct commanding the size and shape to go for, and back again, flitting through the apple and plum trees, a quick glance to make sure she wasn't being observed, down and in.

Did she know that the pigeon had died? Had she spotted the dread sickle of the hunting wing? Had she crouched among the new leaves of the ash tree, as soft lemon as her own throat, frozen with fear, knowing that any movement could give her away? Had she witnessed the unwary young pigeon, only recently fledged, snatched in mid-air, crash to the grass, seen the mad fire in the sparrowhawk's eye? Had those little warbler beads eyed the plucked kill, the hawk mantled over its prey, the bloodied bill, the pale soft feathers drifting on the wind, and noted it all in her warbler memory bank? Or was it chance, just good fortune that feathers of every size and shape were right there, conveniently spread out for her on the mown grass only thirty yards away?

Perhaps that's what warblers do when they arrive here from their long migration from Africa. Perhaps the availability of suitable feathers triggers the nest-building, helps choose the site. Isn't that what we do when we're nesting, when we're moving house? Check out the local schools, the distance to the shops or the bus stop? If the food supply is good and the habitat seems right, perhaps it needs that extra component to fire up the warbler action to nest.

Swallows and house martins can be persuaded to nest with a supply of wet mud of the right consistency. Was it those pigeon feathers that had determined just where the nest would be? Who knows? So many questions; so few answers. For now I am just happy to have found the nest, to have glimpsed her five peppered eggs and marvelled at the intricate beauty of her work. I can watch her now from a discreet distance, check her out every morning and hope to learn a little bit more.

*    *    *

If I close my eyes I can recall in immaculate detail the first nest I was ever shown, even though I can't remember exactly what age I was – four or perhaps five. I was taken by my grandfather's large, loving hand and I remember my own hand lost in his. He understood that all children should learn about nature and led me out into the garden, along a stone-flagged path mossy with age, to a small enclosed lawn surrounded by neatly trimmed box hedges three feet high. There, by gently parting the springy stems of the box, I was encouraged to look into a blackbird's nest. The four blue eggs, 'four freckled ovals of perfect sky, luminous with heat', seemed to stare back at me, an image I can picture as vividly now as all those years ago. Very gently, I was allowed to touch them – something I would not do now. The heat startled me; at that unthinking age, I had no idea about eggs or incubation. Then I was led away to stand quietly and watch the hen blackbird return.

A few years later I was encouraged to collect eggs. With my father I made a small cabinet to hold them with trays of my butterflies and moths pinned to their balsa-wood backing. I had drawers of eggs carefully labelled with date and source, just as I had been taught: 'Starling – hole in stables roof, 10.vi.53'; 'Magpie – very thorny tree, 27.v.54' or 'Blackbird – yew hedge, 16.vi.55'. I adhered strictly to the amateur naturalist's unwritten rules of those days: wait till the bird comes off, don't frighten it; never take more than one egg; take it straight after laying or not at all because you can't 'blow' an egg (the liquid contents removed through a single small hole) with a chick in it; never tell anyone else where the nest is.

Amateur and museum egg-collecting – oology is the study of birds' eggs – was widespread and considered virtuous in Victorian times, an almost genteel pastime, persisting well into the 1950s. For centuries it had been seen as reputable, even educational, a worthy hobby for country boys (no doubt a way of keeping them out of trouble), and many bird books and scientific ornithological volumes of the day freely acknowledged the help and information provided by amateur egg collectors. Of necessity, finding the nests trained you to become an acutely observant ornithologist. John Clare's 'The Green Woodpecker's Nest' could not be more explicit:

> Ive up and clumb the trees with hook and pole
> And stood on rotten grains to reach the hole
> And as I trembled upon fear and doubt
> I found the eggs and scarce could get them out
> I put them in my hat a tattered crown
> And scarcely without breaking brought them down . . .

I was very proud of my collection but, to my dismay, it had to go. Collecting protected birds' eggs, but not possessing a prior collection, became illegal with the passing of the Protection of Birds Act 1954, but it would still, with the exception of a small number of unrelenting obsessives, take a long time for the practice to fizzle out. It was finally endorsed by the Wildlife and Countryside Act of 1981, which made it illegal not only to take but also to possess egg collections.

Back at the turn of the twentieth century, in the very early days of the nature-conservation movement, and when the Victorian obsession for killing wildlife for museum collections was beginning to wane, attention turned to critically endangered species, particularly birds. Egg-collecting was widely practised and accepted, but because it was patronised and supported by such high-profile society figures as the plutocratic zoologist Lionel Walter, 2nd Baron Rothschild of Tring Park, who had created a private natural history museum at his home, it would take several decades to surface as the conservation threat it really was. Only when the Liberal politician and former governor-general of South Africa, Earl Buxton, criticised the practice at a public meeting of the RSPB, warning of the distinct menace posed by egg-collecting members of the British Ornithological Union (of which Lord Rothschild was a prominent member) that pressure began to be brought to bear.

Rothschild and his associates were furious. He joined ranks with another fanatical collector, the widely respected ornithologist the Rev. Francis Jourdain (he of Witherby, Ticehurst, Jourdain and Tucker's *Handbook of British Birds*, first published in 1938), and formed a splinter group calling themselves the British Oological Association, later to be renamed the Jourdain Society after Jourdain's death in 1940. Lord Rothschild, who became famous for driving his carriage harnessed to a team of six zebras to Buckingham Palace to prove that zebras could be tamed and trained, had died a year earlier, still immutably convinced of his egg-collecting contribution to zoology. He is now best remembered for his private museum, which was the largest zoological collection ever amassed by one person. On his death his family gave it to the nation: it is now run by the Natural History Museum, including the largest egg collection in the world of around two million individual eggs.

Yet for a few obsessively addicted enthusiasts it was apparently impossible to give it up. One of the most infamous in recent times was the late Colin Watson, who plummeted to his death in 2006 aged sixty-three after falling thirty-nine feet from a larch tree while prospecting a sparrowhawk's nest. Watson's collection numbered more than two thousand eggs, including osprey, golden eagle, white-tailed eagle, Slavonian grebe, peregrine falcon, merlin, red kite, avocet, corncrake, cuckoo and many other very rare species. He had been caught many times, prosecuted by the RSPB and fined thousands of pounds, to little avail. To this day to a small number of zealots, egg-collecting remains a burning, almost manic compulsion, which can drive them to enormous lengths to evade detection.

Ian Prestt, a former director general of the RSPB, told me the remarkable saga of a well-known obsessive called Edgar Lear, who had been prosecuted several times, and who, the RSPB knew, would never abandon his lifelong fixation. Sometime in the 1960s a pair of wild whooper swans nested on an island in a remote Scottish loch. Such breeding attempts by whoopers are very rare in the UK: the species is migratory and normally breeds in the Arctic. Perhaps one of the birds was unwell and couldn't migrate, or perhaps it was simply aberrant behaviour, as happens from time to time in all animal populations, often spawning whole new colonies.

The RSPB species-protection officers were certain Lear would try to take the eggs, so as soon as the pen swan began to lay, with the help of the local police they mounted a twenty-four-hour guard.

Sure enough, on a drizzly overcast night he appeared in a black wetsuit, creeping through the heather with a specially constructed box strapped to his back. Only a pinpoint of torchlight gave him away. He slipped into the water and swam quietly to the island. The RSPB officers followed the tiny light through binoculars from a distance before closing in to apprehend him as he returned. To be sure of a prosecution they had to catch him red-handed in full possession of the eggs.

Lear was on the island for only a few minutes; then back he came, swimming slowly to the shore with all four eggs – the entire clutch – carefully packed in cotton wool, warm and dry in the little waterproof box on his back, straight into the custody of the officers. The police took him away to be charged and the RSPB men rowed the eggs back to the swans' nest. They stayed only long enough to ensure that the pen went back onto them. Lear was duly charged, appeared before the magistrate, convicted and fined.

Some weeks later the eggs hatched and soon the four fluffy cygnets grew into fine young swans. But something was badly wrong. It quickly became clear that they were not whooper swan cygnets, but common mute swan cygnets with 'S' shaped necks and developing black and orange bills, instead of the straight necks and bright yellow nares of the whoopers.

Lear had known very well that the nest would be guarded and that he was very likely to be caught, but the fervour of his obsession had led him to employ a level of guile even the RSPB had never met before. Earlier that afternoon he had raided a common mute swan's nest somewhere else and put the eggs in his waterproof box. Mute and whooper swan eggs are virtually identical, both large and plain white, slightly pointed ovals – you would need callipers to detect the difference in size. Then he set off on his masterly raid. Once on the island he stole the whooper eggs and quickly buried them in a shallow hole to be recovered for his collection much later. He swam back to the shore, perfectly content to be apprehended.

They didn't know it, but the RSPB officers had been roundly duped. They confiscated the eggs from his box and replaced them in the nest, sure that they had won the battle of wits, that a wicked egg-collector had been caught and that they had ensured the breeding success of the rare whooper swans. They crowed about their prowess, going public with a triumphant press release when Lear was prosecuted. Later, long after the RSPB had ceased to watch the island, Lear returned and recovered his precious whooper eggs for his collection. When, several years afterwards, his house was raided by police, his collection of more than twelve hundred rare birds' eggs was confiscated. There, immaculately blown and labelled, were the whooper eggs.

The Jourdain Society does still exist, but has gone underground and probably only survives as a dining club. Its members have dwindled with age, some now in their eighties, most having received convictions for illegal possession of eggs. A police raid on a society dinner at a Salisbury hotel in 1994 resulted in at least eleven thousand eggs being seized from members' houses around the country. Six members present at that dinner were convicted and fined.

*       *       *

Far out of the reach of egg-collectors are the nests of our goldcrests, the smallest bird on the British list, 30 per cent smaller than the willow warbler, a tiny, febrile jot, an oh-so-little-bit of a warbler weighing just 5–7 grams (less than a quarter of an ounce). If we didn't have a tree-top hide at Aigas I don't suppose I would ever have witnessed a goldcrest nest being made. They spend most of their lives high in the uppermost branches and crowns of conifers, pines, spruces and firs, where they hunt small insects. Their nests are famously difficult to find.

Yet for all their diminutive size, they are strikingly beautiful warblers – if you can ever get close enough to see one properly. The males are principally a pale olive green with the eponymous distinctive orange-flame stripe running back over the crown, fringed with a striking black border against the green of the head. The females are the same, but the stripe is buttercup yellow. When I was a boy they were called golden-crested wrens but, like the willow wren, it was a confusing misnomer. They aren't wrens and the golden stripe is not a crest. Golden-crested warbler would be far too pompous. Goldcrest is much better.

To the boisterous hilarity of visiting school students, last year a pair of swallows nested inside the roof of our tree-top hide, delivering a constant fall-out of chalky white excrement onto the students to shrieks of 'Yeah! Nice one!' and 'Look at Caitlin. Serves you right!' yelled at those unfortunate enough to receive a direct hit. I climbed the thirty-seven steep steps to the hide for the express purpose of meeting the rangers' demands for a 'shit board' to try to contain some of the swallows' fall-out, which was serving as such a distraction to their control of whole classes of eight- to ten-year-olds who found ducking the dive-bombing swallows to be much more fun than learning about the ecological significance of regenerating woodlands.

I fixed the board to the roof beams quickly and easily, then decided to sit for a few minutes to gaze out over the moorland and the glacial valley stretching before me. A sharp-eyed raven floated by, swerving away as soon as it saw me, and a buzzard soared and wheeled lazily high in the blue above. Just as I was about to go I spotted a movement in the verdant foliage of the Norway spruce whose upper branches almost touched the hide. It was a female goldcrest only a few feet away. I sat still. It seemed that she wanted to join me. She edged nearer and nearer in jerky little flits, approaching and then nipping back again when her courage failed her.

After a few minutes of indecision, she entered through one of the seven wide open viewing hatches and flew quickly up into the rafters. She was only there for a few seconds. As she flew out again I noticed a fine filament trailing behind her. It took me a moment or two to understand what she was up to. She disappeared into the foliage of the spruce, but was back again only a minute later. This time I was ready to watch more closely.

Back into the dark confines of the rafters I saw that she was collecting gossamer strands of spiders' web. With another beakful she skipped back into the same spruce frond and disappeared. I quickly moved to a better position and examined the branch through my binoculars. Sure enough she was building a nest in the outermost reaches of the Norway spruce. This intrigued me: I had never seen a gold-crest nest before but, annoyingly, there was one needly spruce frond obscuring my view. I decided to go for a pair of secateurs.

By very carefully leaning out over the thirty-five-foot drop to the forest floor I was able to snip away bits of the offending frond – a minor level of gardening I was sure she wouldn't mind – so that I could see. I was right. In seconds she was inside the hide mining strands of spiders' web once more, then straight back to her nest. This time I could see what she was up to.

You would think it might be safer to nest within the shelter of the tree, closer to the trunk or at least on a sturdy branch. Since the bird is so tiny, and the nest smaller than a tennis ball, built in layers of moss, fine twigs and needles, then whiskery *Bryoria* and *Ramalaria* lichens, all stitched together with spider silk, you would imagine that on an outer frond it would be very prone to being tossed aside or blown out altogether by any forceful gust of wind. Not a bit. This resourceful little warbler is well aware of the risks and takes the precaution of actively guying and binding the nest to the surrounding spruce needles and supporting stem with multiple strands of spider silk (which, I learn, is five times stronger than the equivalent high-grade alloy steel and has the added qualities of flexibility and elasticity in any temperature), weaving it round and round with her tiny bodkin of a bill until she was entirely satisfied the nest was secure.

I was gripped by this macro-ingenuity. There is no end to nature's awesome creativity. I sat transfixed, occasionally ducking the swallows' best efforts to bomb me. Two hours slid past and still she was beavering away, back and forth, in and out, weaving, plucking, pulling and winding, drawing threads like a skilled seamstress, tucking in ends, twisting them off and busying round and round the nest. She was a perfectionist, a precision purist, sometimes pleased with her work so that she could start afresh somewhere else, and sometimes clearly not, unpicking it and starting all over again, nipping back for more silk thread until the result matched the demanding standards of her innate conditioning.

The following day I hurried back to see what more she had achieved. The sun flashed and glinted on the silvery web so that I could see the full extent of her labours. I was dazzled, swept up in this minuscule feat of avian aptitude, this astonishingly deft warbler dexterity. It would have taken a mighty wind to unravel or wrench free that remarkable little orb of a nest. Now both birds were at it, the male arriving with an endearing flurry of wing fluttering and a chatter of thin, high-pitched calls. The female had moved on to the all-important insulation lining of the nest. She still seemed to be doing most of the work, but the male, unmistakable beneath his bright orange flash, was at least bringing in strands of sheep's wool. These she took from him as though she didn't trust him to do the weaving properly. Off he went again. This time he returned with what I could clearly see were two long russet hairs from my Highland cattle, with red shaggy coats and buffalo tough hides. So tough that they delight in scratching on barbed wire, clogging the barbs with the fine russet filaments, long and silky, perfect for goldcrests to weave into the lining of their nests. His female seemed very pleased with these; she sent him off again while she bent to the task of weaving the hair, just as she had done with the spiders' web.

When I returned the next day I could see the almost completed nest. The interior lining was now a mix of tiny feathers bound into the moss and lichen with hair, smoothly and delicately woven. The birds were nowhere to be seen and they never did nest there, although I failed to discover why not. Perhaps, after all, she wasn't satisfied. Had the next class of rowdy school-kids spooked her? Had the swallows dive-bombed her because she was so close to their territory? I will never know. But I came away richer for the instinct-driven little pageant I had witnessed. The industry, the dedication, the skill, the thousands of journeys for materials, the embroidery, the genius of design and construction, the intricacy, the detail and perfection all came together in a triumph of creative brilliance.

Goldcrests live lives of feverish top-spin urgency. They die in droves in the winters because their tiny bodies cannot contain the heat they need to survive. As many as a quarter of the entire population may not survive a harsh winter. To compensate they must lay seven to eleven eggs and always have more than one brood. They hurry. The female often lays a second clutch in another nest while the male continues to rear to fledging the first brood. If the food supply is good and the weather fair, goldcrests are capable of fledging twenty young in the space of two months, but the mortality of young in their first winter is as high as 80 per cent, so they may rear only four of those chicks to adulthood. Because it was well on into June when I found it, I was sure the nest I watched being built was not their first. I prayed that it wouldn't be their last.

# 16

# Summer Night

To see the Summer Sky,
Is Poetry, though never in a Book it lie –
True Poems flee –

'Poem 1472', Emily Dickinson

This is thy hour O Soul, thy free flight into the wordless,
Away from books, away from art, the day erased,

the lesson done,

Thee fully forth emerging, silent, gazing, pondering the themes

thou lovest best . . .
'A Clear Midnight', Walt Whitman

The longest day, the shortest night, the northern hemisphere's pinnacle moment, its apogee, its uttermost fling of solar indulgence. Yes, it's a solstice again, the summer solstice. It's that briefest of exultations when, on our elliptical journey round the sun, the Earth's axial tilt of $23.45°$ tips us, here in the north, into maximum solar radiation. It's what finally announces the arrival of our capricious Highland summer, a summer that may, or very possibly may not, prove to be everything we want.

Yet midsummer's most endearing feature, and the one

that imprints itself on most visitors' memories, is the Highland night. At this latitude, 57°46′43″ North, the Aigas night recedes to under an hour of true darkness on 21 June or, perhaps more meaningfully put, our day – defined by me as the ability to read a newspaper outside – stretches to something approaching twenty-two hours and a few minutes.

The precise statistics for our latitude reveal that on 21 June the sun officially sets at 10.03 p.m. and rises again at 04.28 a.m., a total sunless (but not lightless) gap of six hours and twenty-five minutes. But this is misleading and it's quite wrong to call that a night. The angle of the sun's decline to the horizon is so obtuse and its six-and-a-half-hour passage below the horizon so low that its fiery afterglow continues to beam semi-daylight – the diffuse light of a mildly overcast day – well on into what at any other season would be proper night. Added to this, if it's not cloudy, the sunset bleeds on and on as the sun glides through, inches beneath the horizon, stretching and sliding its reds and purples far into the reluctantly descending darkness. It becomes a Tug o' Light, seeming at first almost to haul the night away altogether. But the Night Team does eventually rally and win through: the daylight finally collapses as if they've suddenly let go of the rope and darkness plummets in, so that you have to abandon reading your newspaper at about eleven thirty. Even so we are still left with a line of gleaming steel along the northern horizon just to prove that the sun hasn't abandoned us altogether. That never goes away, and although you may have given up straining your eyes on your newspaper, be patient, it's not for long.

Night is an illusory pause in the battle, a temporary setback, like an evil thought summarily shamed away by honest conscience, because just a hundred and eight minutes later, by 01.18 a.m., only three and a quarter hours after the sun set, the Light Team is back on the rope with fresh vigour. The sun is lifting, imperceptibly at first, but gradually, as stealthily as a wildcat stalks its prey, it's heading up again, heaving back to the surface. The steely gleam expands and spreads and, before you know it, dawn is arriving.

We've lived with it for forty years, so we're inclined to be blasé about it, almost forgetting it's happening, but our guests from further south are always astonished. 'I can't believe how light it is up here,' I hear, over and over again. 'It's amazing. I didn't want to go to bed', which is precisely what everything else is thinking.

Blackbirds flute their sad notes into still air and robins tick and tinkle thin wisdom as the late-evening light seems to stand still. If the weather is fine and, better still, if it's a full moon, the night is receding before you've had time to fold your newspaper and head back to the house. For the robins and the blackbirds it is a very short sleep. By three in the morning they're at it again, soon to be joined by the whole choral throng: bellowing chaffinches, trilling wrens, grating greenfinches, warbling blackcaps, all mixed in with hooting tawny owls and, if only they hadn't abandoned us this year, the raucous racketing of the rooks out and feeding their fully fledged young.

Yet the real winners are the plants. To be able to photo-synthesise for up to twenty hours a day creates a massive surge in energy available for growth. Combined with the seasonal rise in soil temperature, plants rocket skywards or spread their green solar collectors as far and wide as they can, all of them, from the lowliest photosynthetic algae on a gatepost to the hundred and thirty-year-old sequoias planted by the Victorians, now towering hundred and twenty feet over the house, they're all at it, all surging upward, all expanding, all exposing their leaves for maximum absorption. It's a green revolution after the long months of winter, an explosion of growth and verdure so fast and so unstoppable that, before we can mutter, 'Summer solstice', the gardens are swamped with weeds, broom and gorse banks are bursting with bright yellow blooms, the lawns need cutting twice a week and the roadside verges are spilling hooligan umbellifers into the carriageway.

Studying the statistics again, one more snippet of technical precision grips me and it's one that, in a curious way, defines the whole solstice phenomenon and makes me wonder who on Earth first spotted it and possessed the sensitive instrumentation to measure it. It is this: on 21 June the sun appears almost to stand still. In fact the official difference between the length of day on 20 June and 21 June is a blink of just one second – from 17 hours, 35 minutes and 18 seconds, down to 17 seconds, whereas on the 19th/20th the daylight is still lengthening by 8 seconds a day, and by the 22nd/23rd it has started reducing by 7 seconds a day. All of this is a reflection on our tilt and our elliptical course. Thank God fasting for the gift of that tilt, that wondrous parent of diversification, that miraculous accident of creation that has made us what we are. It hands us our seasons, shapes our

climate, fashions our poles and our tropics, causes our multi-
tudinous migrations, and forges our manifold differences.

\*   \*   \*

At nine o'clock I climb the hill slowly. I'm heading back to
the Iron Age fort, the humped vantage-point seven hundred
feet above the glen where I met the glorious sun-bronzed
roe buck just after the winter solstice. The fort has been a
shapeless heap of boulders for centuries, but long ago its
sturdy walls provided a place of last resort, a sanctuary the
Aigas people ran to when raiders came rampaging through.
Now I go there for escape from the jangling, clamouring
world we all live in these days, for a private sanctuary of
my own, a place where I can commune with the rugged
landscape that has been my home for so long. It's a splendid
look-out high above the valley.

From here I can watch the sun's long decline to the mountains of Glen Strathfarrar in the west, trace its gory trail
north-westwards and follow its fiery afterglow right round
to the north. There is almost always cloud in the west, the
mountains forcing the warm, wet Atlantic air upwards, but
as long as it is thin and distant, this wraith of cloud enhances
the sunset. The sun's fire is reflected back with renewed
vigour, adding depth and authority to the afterglow.

I have come to try to witness the famous 'green or emerald
flash', the sudden surge of green light, which, on rare but
apparently unforgettable occasions, immediately follows the
sun's disappearance below the horizon or precedes its rise.

I have read about it, tried to see it from African deserts and Arctic wastes, but it has always eluded me. I've never witnessed it, although once I narrowly missed it. We were on a Costa Rican beach looking out at the Pacific Ocean, sitting in camp chairs revelling in a fiery sunset. I was distracted by the capuchin monkeys in the trees around our camp, monkeys that watched our every move so that, as soon as we weren't looking, they could nip in and steal anything edible we had been careless enough to leave out. Green flashes were not on my mind. I looked away at the wrong moment but my companion beside me suddenly cried out. I glanced up, but it had vanished.

It is best viewed at sea with a clear, clean horizon, but it can be seen anywhere and it is real, although it's caused by a mirage phenomenon. As the sun disappears, so its rays are fragmented and broken up into the spectral colours of a rainbow. The Earth's atmosphere acts as a weak prism as the rays beam obliquely through, principally refracting blue and green light. The blues are a shorter frequency than the greens and bend themselves out, lost in the atmosphere, leaving, for a fleeting second, the luminous greens dramatically powering into the sky.

Tonight I'm lucky. The auguries are good: no wind, and the sky is clear overhead. I have checked my watch with the internet and I wait calmly for the appointed 10.03 p.m. Although I've climbed to seven hundred feet, the mountains in the west rise to four thousand feet above sea level and the precise timings for this latitude are calculated at sea level, so it's as well I'm here early. The sun's last glimpse, passing from my view, actually fell at 9.51 p.m. It slid behind the slumped pyramid hulk of Beinn a' Bha'ach Ard (two thousand two hundred and twenty-eight feet – which makes it a Corbett – 'hill of the high byre' in Gaelic), setting the whole rim of the mountain ablaze as it went. The afterglow that followed was just what I had hoped for but, alas, no sign of the emerald flash. It was hard to be disappointed because the night was so fine and the sunset promised to be long and poetic. By ten o'clock, I wrote, 'the overall light of day hasn't changed at all'. I had no newspaper, but I could sit and scribble in my journal as easily as if it were midday.

So I sat on a rock with the coconut perfume of gorse and broom flowers lifting from the valley far below, assaulting me from all angles with pulses of heady scent. I sat and wrote for nearly an hour. It was balmy, a June night of calm and tranquillity. Slowly drowsiness claimed me. I lay back with the canvas pad of my notebook's waterproof case under my head – pillow just enough to soften the rock on the back of my skull. The sky above me was a deep, purpling blue, threaded with the same blushing pink of the bell heather just coming into bloom beside me. Before I knew it I was asleep.

When I awoke I was chilled and stiff. I wasn't immediately sure where I was and it took a couple of seconds to remember why I was there at all. I couldn't read my watch; it was too dark. The rock was cold and a touch of dew had beaded the grass at my feet. Cursing my sleepiness I dug for my mobile phone. It said 01.49 a.m. At that moment I wished I was at home and in bed, but not for long.

I have always been partially nocturnal. Lucy has grown

accustomed to me rising in the small hours, standing at the open window, breathing in the night air, or tiptoeing off downstairs and, if the mood is right and the weather is fine, outside for a night stroll. She ignores me now, although years ago it troubled her. 'Where *have* you been?' she used to ask, as I crawled back to bed at 3.30. A question I could never satisfactorily answer. 'Just out and about', was usually the best I could come up with. It's an infection well known to poets, as Longfellow brilliantly expressed in his powerful 'Hymn to the Night'. Nowadays I think Lucy's just glad she hasn't caught it.

> I heard the trailing garments of the Night
>     Sweep through her marble halls!
> I saw her sable skirts all fringed with light
>     From the celestial walls!
>
> I felt her presence, by its spell of might,
>     Stoop o'er me from above;
> The calm, majestic presence of the Night,
>     As of the one I love.
>
> I heard the sounds of sorrow and delight,
>     The manifold, soft chimes,
> That fill the haunted chambers of the Night,
>     Like some old poet's rhymes.
>
> From the cool cisterns of the midnight air
>     My spirit drank repose;
> The fountain of perpetual peace flows there,—
>     From those deep cisterns flows.

Slowly the sleep dulling cleared from my eyes and I was drinking from those 'cool cisterns of the midnight air'. The Highland summer night is soft. It's as smooth as the silk scarves of Rajasthan in the bazaars of old Delhi, and as soft as eiderdown plucked straight from the nests of Icelandic eider farms. It's fresher by far than the sultry air of day. It possesses a new sensual density of its own, charged with nocturnal electricity, each molecule loaded with a static presence that electrifies the senses. It hones awareness, sharpens my hearing, enables me to comprehend its freshness on my face, discern the contractile curtain of my irises widening to Longfellow's 'haunted chambers of the Night'. Time stands still. History and the present merge, the spirit lifts to the moon, a perfect crescent, crisp and close enough to touch. My skin tingles with a new sensory alertness, all cynicism banished, just an anonymous, outpouring openness to the marbled sky. It seems to cling to other presences, things that by day might have completely passed me by – the soft flutter of bats' wings, a moth landing on my sleeve, the secret rustlings of a shrew. With the clarity of gin, an intuition came wading in to take charge, bringing a compulsive intoxication all its own, 'the calm, majestic presence of the Night'.

I hadn't, as I feared, entirely missed the show. The biblical blackness of the mountains stood out clear and hard and the funereal flags of cloud still hung there, but in between the fire had 'smoored', as the old Highlanders would say when they tamped theirs down for the night with moist peat. Still the rim of light clung on, had refused to be over-come. As bright as polished silver, a long, silken ribbon simmered there, rising and falling with a strange, luminous glow. I needed to get higher for a better view.

It's only a twenty-five minute hike from the Iron Age fort up to the trig point height of Bad à Chlamhain at one thousand and four feet ('hill of the red kite'), the imme-diate high point above us at Aigas; a walk I have done hundreds of times and whose boulders and bogs I know well. Walking in the monochrome semi-darkness of moon-light was easy. The going was firm and lichenous over the rocky shoulder of the hill, and wet flushes gleamed like dulled steel as I skirted them. I was approaching from the west, with my back to where the sun had gone down, so for a while I saw nothing of the horizon behind me. Once onto the slope up to the trig point I was in deep heather. Its woody stems brushed my trousers with a swishing sound too loud for comfort. I wanted anonymity and was pleased to emerge into the final boulder field through much shorter vegetation.

Panting, the haul up seemed steeper in the gloom, hands pressing down on knees, chest heaving. I had to stop every few minutes to let my heart subside. That last push, although only three hundred feet, seemed much more than that. It was a relief to come onto the gently sloping lichen heath less than an inch high – the vegetation of all exposed tops in the Highlands – to the summit where the trig point stood out in hard black silhouette. As I did so, the northern horizon came into view.

Breathing deeply I leaned against the cold concrete of the trig. My phone said 02.18 a.m. I placed it on the flat top of the trig and pressed the compass app. The pointer swung smoothly to the north where the tips of a distant spruce plantation stood as sharp and clear as crocodile's teeth. I was surprised to see how much light glowed behind them. I glanced at the time again – 02.23 a.m. I hadn't expected that in the north so soon. A dawn at 04.28 a.m. was fixed in my head: still two hours to go. When I picked the phone up again it felt greasy and I realised that I had inadvertently placed it on fresh bird droppings unseen on the flat top. Hmm, I thought, as I wiped it clean. Something perches here. I settled down to wait for the dawn.

I suppose it was inevitable that I would fall asleep again. For all my alertness and heightened sensitivity, it was the middle of the night. But a two-hour wait was too much. I was comfortable with my back against the sloping concrete, the lichen cushioning my bottom and, with nothing much to look at, 'the trailing garments of the Night' claimed me. I nodded off.

I awoke with a jerk. It was much lighter: dawn had sneaked in around me without waking me. I felt a little foolish, blinking into full unexpected daylight. I sat there waiting for my eyes to adjust and gradually sensed that I wasn't alone. Perhaps it was the slight scrape of its arrival on the trig point that had brought me back to life. Very slowly I turned and looked up. There, with its back to me, was the certain author of the white excrement I had wiped from my phone. It hadn't seen me. Against the lightening sky it was in silhouette, so, snail-like, I eased myself away from the concrete, turning as I did so, until I could see properly who my neighbour was.

A small bird sat there, no bigger than a blackbird, but this was no blackbird. I could see a blue-grey back and long folded wings with tips of jet and a long, slate grey tail, dipped in Indian ink at the very base. My brain screamed, 'Merlin!' Unmistakably an adult male merlin, the smallest of the British falcons; a bird I never, ever get to see close up. Merlins are hunters of meadow pipits and skylarks, chasers-down of unwary tits and siskins crossing open moors. They are fast, determined, unforgiving and fierce. All I usually see is a darting crossbow silhouette against the sky, or a fleeting arrow streaking across the heather, barely time to focus in with my binoculars. Now there was one a yard away, wings crossed behind its back, the early-morning light glinting silver from the top of its head.

A falcon's eyes look directly forward with binocular clarity for sharp focus on the prey it's chasing. Facing away from me, this bird had no idea I was there, would not have detected any movement behind it. It must have perched on that trig point on hundreds of undisturbed mornings; a perfect vantage-point for the first hunt of the day, binocular orbs scanning the moor below, searching for that first unwary meadow pipit to emerge from its heather roost. Why would a merlin think of looking behind the trig? And why on Earth would a human be sleeping there at four o'clock in the morning? A preposterous notion to a falcon intent on a breakfast hunt. Besides, this was his trig point. With an upward flick of his long tail he had claim-marked it with a long white streak. It was his.

I was sitting, knees up, arms resting on them. I froze, my eyes fixed on the bird. I knew that sooner or later he would discover me and I prayed that I would be granted a little longer to drink in his image, his splendid blue jacket and long black primaries. And I wanted to see into his eyes, his large, round black-opal orbs ringed with a thin circle of citrus yellow. He shuffled his wings as if about to take off and then he thought better of it, flicked them once from the shoulders and sprang lightly round as he did so. It seemed that nothing had attracted him to the south, so he would try the north. He was looking straight at me.

Falcons cannot register astonishment. It exists in neither their vocabulary nor their repertoire. All they can do is stare – or perhaps 'glare' is a better word. A glare-stare. A stare of astonishment, a glare of indignation, of outrage, of affront, of how-dare-you irritation, of incredulity, all rolled into one un-frowning, wide-eyed falcon scowl. It was awesome in its diminutive power. I felt I ought to apologise, to back off bowing. Was Merlin the wizard named after the merlin bird, or vice versa? I don't know, but under the spell of that stare it would not have surprised me if I had vanished in a puff of smoke or suddenly found that I was a frog. This was a wizard-bird and a bird-wizard, both. And he was magnificent, perched heraldically upon his personal obelisk, neat, elegant, haughty, commanding and as taut as a bow-string.

I now don't know how long we stared at each other. I'm

sure it was only minutes, but it could have been days, months, years. I have the image now: it's as clear and crisp and captivating as it was that day. I have only to close my eyes and he's there again, still glaring, still commanding. When it ended he gave no hint of alarm or warning. He sprang into the cool morning air, his short pointed wings flicking him away and down round the hill with all the sudden decisiveness of a shooting star. He was gone. I leaped to my feet and ran to the edge, but I was too late. He had vanished. He had skimmed away across the lumpy contours of the heather and the sphagnum where he belonged, lost in the lifting light of the morning.

I turned back to the trig point and stood looking out at the light streaming in from the east. I glanced at my watch. It was 04.37 a.m. The sun was smouldering below the horizon of trees, firing them as if to burst into flame. With a head full of falcon I moved to the edge to begin my careful descent. I looked up for one last time and there it was – a clear, bright emerald flash shot up from the trees and vanished into the silver sky.

# 17

# A Day of Spiders

The spider, dropping down from twig,
Unfolds a plan of her devising,
  A thin premeditated rig
    To use in rising.

And all that journey down through space,
In cool descent and loyal hearted,
  She spins a ladder to the place
    From where she started.

'Natural History', E. B. White

July spilled into August, like a rich, syrupy white wine from the Austrian Burgenland, luxuriant, embracing, irresistible. Early-morning mists now hung over the dark river and the loch, reluctant to leave. Our days were lit with rolling surf of sun-burnished cloud and our nights washed with warm rain as the rowan berries yellowed through to tangerine; by the end of the month they would be scarlet.

Like godly ladies at a church fête, peacock and red admiral butterflies thronged the buddleia blooms, flashing their rococo wings, pushing each other aside to feast on the nectar. In the fields drifts of the little umber and orange-tipped Scotch argus, a seasonal delight in these hills, danced across the candelabrum heads of creeping thistle. At night autumn moths, with names as lovely as their exquisite patterns of mimicry and camouflage, emerged and took to the wing: black rustic, silver Y, antler moth, angle-barred sallow, yellow underwing, bordered beauty, gold spangle. Drawn to the outside lights, they were hawked and feasted upon by a constant fluttering fly-past of soprano pipistrelle bats.

August: the month that gives and takes away. The hovering month, the month that could yet turn out to be a high summer of long, dreamy days, but which will always end in autumn. Whatever the temperature or whatever the hours of sunshine, the days are in retreat, dawns creeping later with the stealth of a wildcat, and the stretch of darkness closing in on us, like a medieval army, herding us inch by inch towards winter whether we notice it or not.

For all its many inducements, I cannot love it. With February, August is stuck fast at the bottom of my score-card of un-favourite months. Its bothersome images are too firmly logged; too many decades have proved them true. The word immediately conjures tiresome midges and flies, sultry nights and muggy days, tourist traffic clogging our single-track roads and the sudden rash of litter spilling out of bins in car parks. But more than all of those, it is also a natural-history hiatus, a fact that strikes at the heart of our daily lives. August cramps our style.

Our loyal field centre rangers have to work much harder to earn their laurels. Long gone are the comfortable days of certainty, knowing where birds are nesting, where the pine martens have a den, where a bank of *Trollius* globe flowers shimmers in the sun. Life has changed for us all. Most of the summer migrant birds have suddenly vanished, finished breeding and fled south. Hard-wired to know what's coming, they have slipped away in the night for the security of food and warmth. The woods and fields are strangely empty. The winter incomers, the ducks, geese and swans from their Arctic breeding grounds, have yet to arrive. Most wild flowers are over; they've melted away as though they were never there at all, and the rude and bully-boy weeds – the bracken, the docks, the rosebay willow herb, the brambles and wild raspberries – have shouldered in and taken over. All subtlety has disappeared and a great green stain has descended across the land.

Nothing looks fresh any more, no breeding plumage – the Slavonian grebes have shed their dinner jackets and marmalade eyebrows, they will be off to the coast any day now, and those red-throated divers as are left on their breeding lochs now deny their name in overalls of workaday grey. No dawn chorus, no blackcap rhapsody or cascading willow warbler any more, even the rooks and jackdaws are reticent, only the robins chinking and tinkling a new pre-autumnal refrain as if to make the point.

It brings out the worst in me; having the Highlands to ourselves for most of the year can make us selfish and irritable when we are forced to share it – the Highlanders have a word for it, 'crabbit'. It turns me introspective with a shoulder-shrugging denial; I don't want to go out. Sometimes it gets to me and I hide away.

In such moods I like to escape to the high pastures, steep fields rank with thistles and rushes, *Rumex* docken stems with dry seed heads burned to Tuscan umber by the summer sun among the multiple florets of ragwort as bright as fresh English mustard, much hated by stock farmers for the toxic sugars in their dried stems if they get swept up in the hay bales.

These high fields have rocky outcrops and hollows where the terrain is too rough or too steep to cut for hay. The lazy grazers have passed them by and the long, coarse grasses have long since gone to seed. Their sere fringes bend to the breezes riffling through like wind on water, and their friendly shuffling stems whisper a perpetual gossip of indecipherable intimacies. I find such corners of accidental wilderness alluring at this pivotal turning of the year. I love to lie down where it's thickest, stretched out on my back, face to the heaving clouds laced with the aerobatic skimmings of swallows and house martins hawking the late summer harvest of flies.

It is here, in these unplanned sanctuaries of wildness, that I can see most clearly what has gone so badly wrong with the British countryside. If I turn my face to the forest of stems and lie still, within the space of one minute I can witness the full spectrum of summer fecundity we now unkindly and dismissively lump together as 'biodiversity'. This accidental savannah is a long way from its prosaic generalisation, and August seems to be its apogee. It is uncountably rich in insects, flies, ants, bugs, beetles, spiders and other invertebrates, a bustling, crawling throng as busy, colourful and varied as a medieval bazaar. By lying still and just surveying the stems in my immediate vision I can quickly count a dozen different species from as many diverse families, many of which I cannot name. There are froghoppers, lacewings, ladybirds, grasshoppers, spiders and harvestmen, weevils, aphids and leafhoppers, ground bugs and mirids. I would need a week with an expert to begin to sort them all out.

Turning to the sky again, overhead, flitting among the softly waving seed heads are tiny brown diurnal moths, dancing butterflies, hoverflies and gnats, and then the occasional bumble bee comes barrelling through. There is nothing romantic about this superabundance of invertebrate life, nothing of the buttercup-twirling rural idylls of *Cider with Rosie* or *Akenfield*; nor is it an elegiac reflection of a former agricultural existence, although it has its place in any corner of undisturbed countryside. No, rather it is simply what nature properly is when, either on purpose or by accident, man eases back the pressure, steps aside and allows it to happen.

It is a sad fact that corners of unkempt wildness, such as here at Aigas, are rare in the British countryside today. We are not a nature *reserve*. We haven't set land aside or specifically ring-fenced it for any species or habitat, but we do our best to respect all of nature's functions and we just let things happen on their own. We avoid all chemicals – weed killers are banned, as are chemical fertilisers – and cattle- and sheep-stocking levels are sympathetic to our land and its vegetation. We favour permanent pasture fertilised by cow dung and the die-back of its own grasses and weeds. We don't drain the wet flushes. We leave the stinging nettles for butterflies. We go light.

As a result, nature takes over and builds its jungles and forests. Fungus churns invisibly in the soil and humus assembles its own working capital. The cattle drift through. Their emery tongues rasp and tear, loosening roots. Their liquid dung is tart with precious nitrogen and the softer ground is pitted and pierced by their heavy cleaves. Dung flies and beetles motor in. Nutrients disperse in the rain. Invertebrates of myriad species find a home, breed and disperse. It isn't wilderness, but it is a doffed hat to nature's grand ambitions, a chance for bugs and birds, mice and voles, weasels, stoats, brown hares, foraging badgers, opportunistic pine martens and the omnipresent wild deer to stake their claims.

★   ★   ★

Sitting at my desk one morning I looked up to see a thin veil of smoke passing the window. Puzzled, I rose and walked across the room to the bay window that looks out over the river fields. Normally I can see right across the glacial valley to the forested hills on the other side, the river glinting in between. That morning I could barely see the far side at all. It couldn't be smoke, I reasoned, there was too much of it. It must be drifts of low cloud. Then it cleared and handed back the view.

I returned to my desk. A few moments later I noticed it again; another pale shroud passing on a gentle south-westerly breeze, funnelling along the valley. But something wasn't right. Late summer mists don't do that, they hang, and anyway, the cloud base was high. Perhaps it was smoke, after all. I got up again and stood in the window just as another cloud closed off my view. I always keep my precious Swarovski binoculars on my windowsill so I took a closer look.

What I saw was a breath-taking spectacle of such over-whelming natural abundance that I was lost for words. I picked up the phone to Ian Sargent, our field officer, who was off duty with his girlfriend Morag Smart, who ran our schools programmes. 'Come quickly. You must see this.' As always, when I stumble across some extraordinary natural phenomenon, my first instinct is to share it. But I also wanted witnesses. The world is full of cynics. I knew people wouldn't believe me if I kept it to myself.

It was neither mist nor smoke. It was silk. Spiders' web silk. The massed gossamer threads of millions of tiny spiders dispersing by a process known as 'ballooning'. Every long grass stem, every dried dock head, every tall thistle, every fence post held, at its apex, a tiny spiderling – what we commonly know as a money spider – poised, bottom upturned to the wind in what has been described as the 'tiptoe position' and from which single or multiple threads of silk were being spun. Other spiders were queuing beneath, awaiting their turn. As each slowly lengthening thread caught the wind we could watch the spider hanging on, tightening its grip on the stem or the seed head, while the gently tugging threads extended ever longer into the breeze.

For the tiniest spiders lift-off happened when the threads were ten or fifteen feet long, but slightly larger spiders spun for much more – perhaps twice that length. Then they let go. The spiders were airborne, sailing gently up, up and away across the fields, gaining height all the time, quite literally ballooning down the valley with the wind.

The pure physics of this feat is best demonstrated by holding up a long length of ribbon on a windy day. The ribbon is never straight. It bends and buckles, folds and twists and tugs at your hand with the turbulence of the wind. The constantly changing contours of the silk thread give it the lift and the mobility, providing sufficient sail to carry the weight of the tiny spider. The longer the threads, the more lift and sail they provide. Whether the spider knows instinctively when to let go, or whether it is dragged off when the pull of the thread gets too great for its grip, I have no idea. Perhaps the spider hasn't either.

What I do know is that while this is a well-known and widely practised mechanism for spider dispersal across many *Arachnid* families, it only very rarely happens in such vast and impressive multitudes. The valley was full of silk. Surely not by intent the millions of gossamer threads collided and entangled, creating ever bigger and more effective sails as they drifted down the wind. It would be almost too much to ask of natural selection for an organism to have evolved not just to best-guess the weather, but also somehow knowing in advance that by a simultaneous release of silks its species could enhance the efficacy of their dispersal mechanism, creating a collective sail for hundreds of thousands of spiders together. So, until someone convinces me otherwise, I conclude that the extraordinary coagulation we witnessed was accidental, a freak of timing and the weather conditions of the morning. Freak or not, it was astonishing. Whole zeppelins of money spiders were heading east towards Inverness.

The three of us walked silently through the fields in unqualified awe of this phenomenal natural undertaking. I had by then lived at Aigas for more than thirty years – thirty years of looking out over those fields. I had occasionally seen a few spiders ballooning; sometimes landing on me or their threads tickling my face, and I had marvelled at it, but never before had I witnessed anything like this uncountable host of such biblical proportions.

Ian and Morag were awestruck too. We had no words for it beyond the occasional fatuous exclamation of 'Good God!' or 'Look at this lot coming now!' Ian had brought his camera and was busy capturing macro-images of the tiny spiders reversing up to the tip of the grasses, gracefully balancing into the tiptoe position and the silk beginning to emerge from their tail ends. Morag and I stood and gazed out over the fields, over the valley.

It's impossible to estimate the numbers of individual sails we saw that morning. There were millions, perhaps hundreds of millions, maybe billions – I have no idea and I cannot imagine a mechanism for counting them. But I do know that each individual thread was virtually invisible to the human eye at a distance of ten yards. From my study window to a central position above the valley fields is easily two hundred yards, three hundred – even more. For the sails to be so numerous and so thick as to be clearly visible, like a cloud of mist, from considerable range means there must have been countless millions of spiders all ballooning at the same moment, not just in our fields, but many other fields up and down the valley, the air so thick with them that they blotted out the view.

After a while I returned to my study and my desk. But my brain had not been able to assimilate properly what I had just seen. I found that I had to get up over and over again to watch this spider float-past still massing across my gaze. It went on for two and a half hours. When I could no longer see the gossamer clouds I went back down to the field and searched. I couldn't find a single spider. They had all gone.

So why? And what mysterious signal had triggered this mass exodus of spiderlings across the landscape? The tiny spiders we saw were immature *Linyphiid* money spiders, of the common genera *Lepthyphantes* and *Erigone*, both given to the practice of ballooning dispersal. They must also have been hard-wired to recognise precisely the best conditions for this pivotal moment in their tiny new lives. It is inconceivable that so many millions could have communicated with each other over such a huge area, but if the atmospheric pressure, the wind, the humidity and the temperature all came together at the peak moment in the year for *Linyphiid* money spider dispersal, delivering a universal 'Yes, go for it!'

signal to every spider of the right genus and species throughout the valley fields, then it seems likely that meteorology alone could have been the trigger.

Using fans and wind tunnels, scientists have tested air flow as the trigger in laboratory conditions. Results are pretty conclusive. It is consistent air flow that matters most. The correct level and duration of air flow, at the right temperature, stimulated the initial climbing behaviour up the stem of the take-off plant. There was then a pause while the spiders seemed to be assessing the reliability of the air flow before they started spinning silk. After a few minutes, apparently convinced, they assumed the tiptoe position and commenced spinning especially fine threads, sometimes single, sometimes multiple.

Once they are up and away they are totally out of control, literally wafted on the winds of chance. Many will perish; they will land in water and drown, be gobbled by birds, get blown out to sea or into wholly unsuitable habitats. But others, perhaps even the majority, will find suitable pastures new. Some will travel only a few yards, some a mile or two, others may get swirled up into the jet stream and carried round the globe, a fact remarkably illustrated by one tiny South Atlantic island.

The devastating 1961 volcanic eruption of Queen Mary's Peak on the island of Tristan da Cunha caused the evacuation of the entire population of 230 people. The scalding lava flows wiped out all existing life across huge swathes of the island, caused the sea to boil and rendered the land a fiercely hostile desert of caustic ash. When, after several months of cooling, a scientific expedition arrived to assess the damage they were astonished to find that South American *Linyphiid* spiders had arrived on the wind and re-colonised the island. The Argentinian coast is 2088 miles away. They had ballooned in on the turbulent winds of hopeless odds, dropping out of the sky to find themselves accidental first-time colonists. In order for those random few to have made it, millions more must have perished in the ocean.

I have no idea where my spiders landed. Some, I'm sure, achieved only the end of the field or the line of trees at its margin, but that wasn't what mattered to me. It was the overwhelming spectacle of their massed legions, the unassailable conviction in their singular marches up the stems, the unswerving certainty of their resolve, their uninstructed dedication to the species' cause and the astonishing hordes of their silken outpourings clotting the sky that gripped me that day. A day never forgotten.

# 18

# Gods of the Morning

Most satisfying is the robin . . . its song is a fixture of this time of the day. It bubbles up out of the black mass of our hedge like a tiny breeze-ruffled brook of notes. It's the first god of the morning.

*Crow Country*, Mark Cocker

There is blood on the snow
and a trickle of rowan berry juice
on his bib where the pine marten
stands for a moment like a man.

'The Pine Marten', David Wheatley

We have arrived at 15 September and the cycle of our year is almost complete. Today dawned calm, chill but not cold, and as fresh on the cheeks as a splash of cologne. We love this intermezzo in the year's turning. It's pivotal, a point around which everything out there knows it's about to change but drags its feet as if it doesn't want to. It's as though the month is orchestrated by a conductor who can't make up his mind. The weather oscillates, bearing autumn's name yet still trailing a waning summer's coat. Even the air seems to be lingering.

Yesterday the sun beamed its failing warmth across us

with a radiant smile. When I was sitting still in the garden after lunch with my eyes closed, it could easily have been August. Bumble bees hummed and a robin sang deliciously from a cherry tree. Peacock and red admiral butterflies still fluttered through the herbaceous borders and in the shade of the trees midges danced through caves of cool air.

These fleeting moments of the year are among those I cherish most. Before the equinoctial gales sweep in from the west and night temperatures crash to ground frosts that sugar the morning lawns, there are great riches to celebrate and some to avoid. The mysterious world of fungus shows its hand. All year mycelium has been invisibly insinuating its dark authority underground; suddenly it decides to spread its spores. Fruiting bodies emerge from nowhere, bursting out of tree trunks or levering the earth aside mole-like to surface and spread their delicate gills and pores. An hour's fungal foray garners an astonishing array of colours, textures, shapes, varieties and possibilities. The inverted apricot umbrellas of chanterelles, *Cantharellus cibarius*, and sticky brown-capped penny buns or ceps, *Boletus edulis*, are common and mouth-wateringly abundant.

Eugenia, our creatively inspired field centre cook, heads off into the birch woods with a trug over her arm and a rapturous smile herding her cheeks up under twinkling eyes. In her native Poland, edible fungus is a cultural imperative greedily awaited every autumn. This is her moment. She will arrive back with her trug brimming over with chanterelles, ceps and field mushrooms. She will sauté them in butter and deliver up steaming bowlfuls, succulent, aromatic and utterly delicious. They will appear in soups, stews, quiches, omelettes and, most delectably, in scrambled eggs. Those she doesn't use fresh she will dry or bottle in vinegar, hoarding them on a top shelf for the dark days of winter. In the woods and fields at Aigas, we have recorded many hundreds of species of this most arcane form of life.

Not all are so benevolent. Many are parasites, eventually killing off their tree hosts, like the dreaded *Armillaria mellea*, honey fungus, which gives off a deceptively benign honey aroma, and its equally sinister sister species *A. ostoyae*, both of which enhance their menacing presence with radioactive bootlace-like mycelium, which rots the roots of mature trees so that the tree topples in a gale, often snapping off at ground level. What had at one moment appeared to be a tall, healthy tree in the prime of life is suddenly brought crashing to the ground without any warning. When this first happened to a gnarled old rowan tree in the middle of the lawn, I went out on an overcast night and found the exposed black boot-laces of mycelium glowing in the dark with a dull bio-luminescence and the scent of honey floating on the cool night air. They seemed to me to be gloating, smugly pleased with the grim and devastating consequences of their devi-ousness, like a Machiavellian politician of the Renaissance. It would not have surprised me if I had heard a hollow, mocking laugh.

Examining its work in the light of day, I found that I could push my finger into what should have been solid ligneous root tissue – some of the strongest wood in a tree – now reduced to mush. It has accounted for many fine trees around us, rowans, birches, red oaks, sycamores and cherries. I don't know it's there until the mushrooms appear, clusters of bulging, ginger-brown caps thrusting upwards and outwards from the base of the doomed trunk, shoving each other aside in their haste to expand their gills and spread their mellifluous infection of invisible, dust-like airborne spores.

Others are not so devious, but nonetheless devastatingly poisonous if eaten. *Amanita virosa*, the aptly named 'destroying angel', pops its pretty little head up in the shade of its beech tree hosts every autumn, all smiles and innocence, delicately appealing, pure white and chastely veiled like a bride; almost worse, at a cursory glance, when it first appears it is scarily like a field mushroom. But, beware, it is deadly. Mycologists say don't even put it in the same basket with edible mushrooms and wash your hands after touching it. Ingestion of even a small part of one will annihilate your liver and kidneys in a matter of hours. Rapid organ transplant is the only way of surviving the virulent α- and β-*amanatin* toxins.

There are others out there, too: the attractively red-capped, white-spotted fly agaric, *Amanita muscaria*, sometimes known as the Enid Blyton toadstool, grows everywhere here, although its poison is far less threatening. Its toxin, *muscarine*, is hallucinogenic, but don't try it. It can make you very, very ill. And there is the inoffensive-looking *Cortinarius rubellus*, the lethal webcap, a mushroom-sized cinnamon-coloured toadstool with a Chinese coolie's hat that has recently devastated a family not very many miles away from us here. They await kidney transplants and are lucky to be alive.

Eugenia is also to be seen emerging from a thicket or from under a hedge, hair in knots and tangles as wild as the undergrowth, where she has been collecting nature's free fruits. Wild raspberries, blackberries, elderberries and the tiny little flavour-rich wild strawberries all find their way into her trug, then into her jams, her purées and sauces, and will grace her sponge cakes and muffins.

As the first streaks of colour creep into the foliage, as the bracken turns to rust and the deergrass, *Tricophorum cespitosum*, the common, wiry grass of the acid upland slopes, lends a ginger wash to our hill ground, so the rowan trees are burdened with tight bunches of berries as blazing scarlet as a harlot's lipstick. In a week or two they will be stripped bare by migrating thrushes, fieldfares and redwings from Scandinavia, undulating in chattering hordes across our hills and glens in their tens of thousands, but for now they attract an unusual marauder. Eugenia will collect baskets of the berries to boil down and render into rowan jelly, a mildly tart accompaniment for venison, other game such as grouse, woodcock and duck and, best of all, with good old-fashioned mutton. She will produce dozens of jars of the bright orange-pink jelly, a supply to keep us going all year. But it is not Eugenia's depredations on the brightly adorned trees that I am referring to.

No one expects a carnivore to have a passion for fruit, especially not a fruit that appears to be so unpalatable. To the human tongue rowan berries are almost impossible to eat raw. The soft red flesh produces a bitterness as sharp and dry as a crab apple, so sour and with a grimacing aftertaste that even when you have quickly spat them out, your soft palate is left cringing. No one in their right minds would eat rowan berries off the tree. For Eugenia's jelly they need to be rendered down, the seeds strained out, then boiled again with oodles of sugar and the same quantity of cooking apples before the bittersweet juices coagulate into a surprisingly delicate and piquant flavour.

No such delectation for the pine marten. He takes his berries raw off the tree – and he gorges on them every September. We don't really know why this is, but it seems likely that they are a very rich source of vitamin C, which may be lacking in their diet if other mammal prey, such as field voles, are in short supply. Pine martens are omnivores despite their pointedly carnivorous dentition. It is well known that peanuts and strawberry jam will attract them to bird tables and they are known to consume large quantities of bilberries as well as other fruits.

On our bird tables I have tried them on many different foods: rhubarb crumble, apple pie, fruit cake, roast potatoes, baked beans and much more. They take the lot. Once in a week of vicious winter frost I took a hunk of stale fruit cake out for the starving blackbirds to pick at. No sooner had I placed it on the table than a marten popped out from under a bush, leaped onto the table, grabbed the entire hunk and made off with it back into the undergrowth, all while I was still standing there.

I recently took off with Alicia, our staff naturalist, to

explore some rowan trees up in the woods to see to what extent they had been raided by martens. We examined about twenty trees, all laden with dense clusters of fruit. Seventeen of them had been raided. The problem for the martens is that, although they are excellent climbers, the fruit grows on the extremities of the slender branches, too far out and too slender to carry the weight of the marten. So it has to climb up, get as close as it can, bite the twig off so that it falls to the ground, then nip down and feast on the spoils. Most of the trees we examined had a ring of scattered berries and stripped clusters around them. I had never witnessed this happening, but I have seen the consequences virtually every year, immediately followed by little piles of marten faeces deposited in prominent places on paths, on gateposts, on boulders. They are unmistakable: the rowan berries are only partially digested and clearly pass through the martens at high speed, looking more like a vomited bolus than faeces – a rowan purge. This intriguing behaviour will continue for as long as the berries are available on the trees.

What it suggests to me is that the martens may have difficulty in obtaining as much live mammal prey as they would like. Certainly, having witnessed them chasing red squirrels through the trees, and seeing the squirrels outwit and out-climb them on many occasions, I can well imagine that it is inefficient to expend so much energy on the chase. Field vole populations famously soar and then crash. In lean years, the martens may not be able to get as many as they need to supply them with the essential vitamins taken in by the voles in their catholic and seasonally variable diet. Also, of course, the hand of man is in this. Farm fields and dark commercial forests are famously devoid of small mammal prey driven out by monoculture and the application of fertilisers and pesticides. It is just possible that because we have so manipulated the natural habitat of pine martens, their feeding habits have been forced to change towards a more omnivorous diet. If so, that constitutes an intelligent survival shift for the species. When the autumn bonanza comes along perhaps some arcane metabolic alchemy is telling them to gorge on the vitamin-rich berries while the going is good.

★     ★     ★

When I came to live in the Highlands in 1968 the pine marten was a very rare mammal, largely restricted to the remote north-west Highlands. I so well remember the excitement of seeing one for the first time. Traditional persecution was falling away. There were fewer gamekeepers on the land and, most significantly of all, in the late 1970s the Forestry Commission took the controversial decision to cease 'vermin' control on its land – no more employing trappers, no more fox snares, no more men with guns patrolling their woods; this at the same time as an annual planting-target driven expansion in commercial woods right across the uplands.

The resulting dramatic increase in commercial forestry during the 1970s, 1980s and 1990s undoubtedly helped pine martens by providing relatively undisturbed sanctuary and an accidental ready food supply. In those days new plantation forests were established by deep ploughing, the young trees elevated above surrounding weed competition by being planted on top of the turned furrow at the same time as draining the ground. It also laid the substrate bare, broke through cloying, water-retaining peat and revealed minerals. As always, nature motored in and exploited this new opportunity. Grasses, weeds and other nutritious plants sprang up on the naked sides of the furrows. Field voles followed the surge of new growth.

During the establishment stage of new plantations, before the canopy closed off the sun, the voles thrived on the turnover of nutrients, the fresh grasses and other plant food. In some plantations there were vole plagues immediately following planting and for the first few years afterwards. Predatory birds, such as hen harriers, short-eared owls, barn owls, buzzards and kestrels, all benefited from the vole glut and pine martens were likely beneficiaries too, especially where new plantations were created beside more mature ones, providing both sanctuary and an increased food supply. As is so often the case when several ecological factors merge simultaneously, dramatic results occurred. Here, the convenient combination of a sudden marked reduction in persecution, the presence of a vole glut and the dark sanctuary of new forests greatly advantaged the pine marten. Their numbers rapidly increased.

Martens are still limited in their range, but they have spread south and east throughout the Highlands and down into Fife and the Central Belt, even to the outskirts of the great Glasgow conurbation. Here, in these glens of the northern central Highlands, they are now widespread, even common. It is no longer a rare sight to see one dead on the road – a sure indication of a mobile population currently estimated at between three and four thousand animals.

Alicia tells me at present we have four or five individual martens occupying our ground on a more or less permanent basis. For several years she has been awarding them names according to the characteristics of their pelage: Spike, Blondie, One Spot, Thumbs, Patch and so on. Some stick around for several years, others seem to disperse quickly, or perhaps get killed off on the roads or by the few people in the glen who don't like them because they raid hen runs, if they can. Our resident martens den in the stables' roof and occasionally in the lofts of estate cottages and outhouses. I am often amazed by their ability to find a tiny entrance hole under eaves. Our field centre guests love to see them from the hides and are happy to sit out the long summer evenings waiting for them to come in to a bait of peanuts and jam.

*       *       *

It is dawn, the moment in the day I have always loved most. It's a long-standing obsession and it hauls me out, out and about, often doing nothing in particular, just enjoying watching the light lift and the world around me pulling on its clothes for the day. September dawns are often still and cool with a tang of freshness all their own. Mists hang motionless over the river fields. The only bird singing is the ubiquitous robin, tinkling his gentle, melancholic aria that always presages the first light of day. Mark Cocker has called the robin 'the first god of the morning'. He is right.

Each morning I let Lucy's twenty-eight chickens out by pulling the cord that lifts their hatch. One by one they tiptoe into the new day with mildly bemused expressions, slightly lost, as though such a thing has never happened before, rather like inexperienced travellers getting off at an unfamiliar railway station. Then something seems to click and they remember where they are and what to do. With a flap and a scratch they head straight into pecking mode without any of the wary looking round you might expect of a bird so regularly ravaged by furtive, dawn-slinking predators. I throw them a scoopful of grain to reward them for their patience.

Not so the two cockerels, Saddam and Bashar, who have been out-crowing each other for the past hour from within the cobwebby, ammonia-choking darkness of their hut. Every morning their muted cries invade my surfacing consciousness an hour before dawn. Letting them out spins them into a frenzy of territorial crowing, strutting, shaking of blood-red combs and floppy wattles, fluffing out of neck feathers and extravagant tails. It is as though their rampant avian masculinity had been shut down for the night indoors and is suddenly and alarmingly Jack-in-a-box released. They become sexual tyrants, leaping on top of unsuspecting, innocently corn-pecking hens, treading them to the ground and forcing them into sudden cloacal embraces they cannot possibly have seen coming – rooster rape, by any other name.

For once I haven't got the Jack Russells with me. I sneaked

out earlier than usual, leaving them snoring in their baskets beside the Aga. I will return for them later. This gentle autumn has recently produced some glorious dawns and sunrises of candyfloss clouds and still, echoing air. I wanted to be out there without the intrusive bossiness of the dogs, on my own, free to follow my nose and my instincts. I walked quickly away from the hens' paddock and turned up the old avenue of limes and horse chestnuts, picking my way through the prickly shells of fallen conkers on the path. When they land some of them split open, revealing the deep amber shine of the seed socketed into its fleshy cup, reminding me of the liquid eye of a big old shire horse I once knew.

Last year's leaves crinkled underfoot, now with a light scattering of new ones in pastel green and grapefruit yellow, the early fallers of an autumn slow to mature. If we get a sharp frost, in a week or two's time this path will be so thick with drifts of fresh leaves that I will have to wade through them. The big limes and chestnuts have something approaching three million leaves each. The avenue has eleven evenly spaced trees on either side, each 140 years old, planted by the Victorians to line a carriage drive now long disused. Before winter sets in they will deliver to the ground a snow-fall of over sixty million leaves. Little wonder the soils are so rich. Leaf litter, we call it. If only human litter were so universally beneficial to the world.

I crossed the burn on the little bridge where the water from the high moor, brandy-wine brown, gossips a private conspiracy between mossy stones, hurrying down to lose itself in the dark deeps of the Beauly River. There is something profoundly reassuring about a stream. Although the water is simply adhering to the laws of physics, its many moods award it a complex personality as rich as any human being's, at the same time being utterly dependable, far more than many people I know. It is a constant, always there, whether loud or muted, friendly, angered, even outraged in times of spate. It's not in a hurry today but it's difficult to pass over and I stand on the bridge for a moment or two, smiling inwardly.

Just then I got the overpowering sense that I was not alone. I have experienced it many times before and I've long since given up trying to explain it. If it is a sixth sense, I cannot define it beyond observing that it is seldom wrong and I value it greatly. Like a line from a cheap thriller, I feel someone's eyes drilling into the back of my head. I turned slowly. At first I couldn't see anything and thought I must be mistaken, but then, as pure and shocking as coming downstairs and finding a stranger in your kitchen, our eyes meet. Only ten feet away and at my eye level, a pine marten, the size of a slender cat, was perched upright in the central fork of a rowan tree beside the burn. His black front paws rested on a diagonal branch and his long, elegant tail floated below. He was staring straight at me. I was rooted. How long had he been watching me? Why hadn't he run away? Why had he let me get so close? What secret tapes were fizzing inside that tight little torpedo of a skull?

He was magnificent. His head was angular and pert, the sharp little face reflecting a sharper intelligence within. His ears were small and rounded, pale-rimmed at the top. His wet nose gleamed in the morning light. Dressed from head to tail in velvet suiting of dark chocolate, a V-shaped bib ran down his chest and between his forelegs, a bib as rich and glowing as apricot cream. A single spike-shaped smudge of cocoa at the bottom of his bib gave him away. I know this marten. Alicia named him Spike when he first appeared at one of the hides, a fine, full-grown dog marten we see often, a marten with pizzazz, who visits the hides and has been around for a couple of years. Unblinking, his eyes were as bright and beady as polished jet.

A pine marten's life is simple. They are driven by need and fear – those two. Need for food and a mate; fear of man, the dread predator, the exterminator. Occasionally a golden eagle, swooping unseen from high above, will catch a marten out in the open; shreds of fur or a fierce-toothed skull turn up in eyries from time to time, and just occasionally, very rarely, martens fight among themselves and one gets so severely mauled that it wanders off to die, but nothing approaches the threat humans have historically posed. They have been trapped for their shining fur, as soft as mink, they've been shot for stealing hens, gamekeepers have poisoned them for taking game, and we run them over on the roads; not so long ago our efforts drove them to the very edge of doom.

He hasn't moved.

So here we are: the man and the marten. I'm glad he doesn't know that we have persecuted his kind to extermination throughout most of Britain and I'm glad that in this stretched moment of frozen exchange he doesn't yet see me as so dire a threat as to trigger instant flight. The seconds tick by. My eyes are locked on his – his on mine. I'd like to say that it's a game of who will flinch first, but just at this moment I'm not so sure. My brain has emptied down, nothing to offer. For as long as it will last, time has stopped. Spike is glaring at me, like an angry drunk at the other end of the bar, daring me to look away.

Very slowly I withdraw my wits from his metallic, levelled gaze. I know why he is there. It is a rowan tree. This is his time for gorging on rowan berries and he does not like to be disturbed. He has been to the top of the tree and several weighty clusters of fat, ripe fruit lie scattered on the ground between us. He was on his way down to get them, now caught in the act. He wants those berries. Something in the core of his being is telling him he needs them. I think his mouth must be watering. His dilemma is twofold: to come on down for the spoils, or let discretion win and flee, to leap away through the trees as fleet as a squirrel. If he ventures down to get the fallen berries he must come closer to me. If he flees he could be gone in a flash of chocolate fur. He can see those berries; they are his. I know that if I move even an inch, he will go. Indecision and indignation have clashed in his feisty marten brain. For the moment it is stalemate.

I have seen martens on countless occasions, far too many encounters to remember any but the most exceptional, but I have never been fixed by a glare like this before. It is as though I am no longer in control and I have to wait for his next move. The chess analogy is irresistible: I have to wait;

that is the rule of the game. We could be here for a while.

His gaze never flickers and I can't read it. Past experience dictates only one realistic option: that his nerve will eventually fail and he will turn and vanish into the trees. After all these years of seeing and thinking I understood pine martens, I would have put good money on it. Oh! We are so smug. We gain a little familiarity and a little knowledge and we think we've got it sorted. It's all good interesting stuff, this wildlife, but we humans are the superior beings, the smart-arses who boast about wildness as though it is a commodity, something we have invented for our own pleasure and can dabble with as we please. We think that wildlife behaves as it always does, predictable and presumed – you can tempt it in with a bait, trap it, radio-tag it, catch it on camera, plot it on a graph and check it all out in a book. In so far as we're prepared to concede that other species have wills of their own or possess cognitive intelligence, we insist that they are locked within the limitations of their species' hard-wiring. All we have to do is read the wiring and we're home and dry. Job done. We think we know the pine marten.

We are so reluctant to acknowledge that wildness is a quality we humans only vaguely comprehend, that it isn't exclusively ours to do with as we please and that it also embraces other human dimensions, such as wonder, enchantment and rapture, the unpredictable, the illogical, the sensual, the spiritual. Science is about exploring, measuring and testing things. It is also very good at dismissing things it can't check out with an experiment. Enchantment and joy are not so readily assessed. I was enjoying this encounter, no doubt about it. But the smugness of our own imprinting was wrapping me round like a fog. I had fooled myself into thinking my superior brain was back in control. Just a matter of waiting – yes, a game of who will blink first, and I was in charge. And it *would* be Spike, as I had made up my mind it must be. But that wasn't how Spike saw things this morning. Something entirely other was fizzing through the hot cloisters of his acute little brain. What I hadn't understood, hadn't even considered an option, was that this long needly stare was a carefully calculated musteline risk-assessment. It was as though he had sussed that I wasn't going to give in – had weighed it all up and was carefully considering his options, plotting his final move, his check mate. Not in a week of waiting would I have been able to predict what happened next.

Without the slightest hint of panic or hurry he turned away and disappeared down the far side of the trunk of the rowan. Ha! I thought. I've won. I was wrong. Oh! I was wrong, wrong, wrong. There was nothing hard-wired about this second god of the autumn morning. He appeared again at the foot of the tree and in three quick bounds he came straight towards me. From only five feet away a chittering yell of abuse broke from his throat, hurled at me with all the contempt he could muster. Then he snatched up a bunch of berries – his berries – threw me a disdainful glance and vanished back into the undergrowth.

# 19

# Arthur and the Treecreeper

If you wish your children to think deep thoughts, to know the holiest emotions, take them to the woods and hills, and give them the freedom of the meadows; the hills purify those who walk upon them.

*Nature Essays*, Richard Jefferies

He ought to give himself up to a particular landscape in his experience; to look at it from as many angles as he can, to wonder upon it, to dwell upon it. He ought to imagine the creatures there and all the faintest motions of the wind. He ought to recollect the glare of the moon and the colours of dawn and dusk.

*The Man Made of Words*, Scott Momaday

I'm out with a torch. I have done this little nocturnal expedition many times over many years. Tonight I have a companion who is here exploring nature with me for the first time. He is young and keen and lives a long way away, so we don't often get the chance. He is my grandson, Arthur, just five years old, still young enough to sit on my shoulders, which is good because what we are out to see is eight feet off the ground.

I'm taking Arthur to see some huge trees called giant sequoia (*Sequoiadendron giganteum*), famous for their impressive size, their very long lives – some over three thousand years in their native California – and their thick, spongy bark, which evolved as a protection against natural fire, so soft and spongy that you can punch it without hurting your fist. The name 'sequoia' is a corruption of Sequoyah (1770–1840), a celebrated Cherokee Indian jeweller who became famous for creating a Cherokee syllabary and teaching his tribe to read and write. The sequoia we're heading for is one of six fine specimens, exactly a hundred and thirty-six years old, and, vying with the Douglas firs, at over a hundred and sixty-nine feet, among the tallest trees in the Highlands (the tallest is a Douglas at two hundred and nine feet). They were planted with most of the rest of the compact eight-acre Aigas arboretum of fifty exotic and native species when, in 1877, a grandiose Victorian extension was being built onto the front of the much more modest Georgian (1760) House of Aigas. It was the fashionable thing to do – more than that, it was almost mandatory, mandatory, that is, if the owners were to achieve the social status they almost certainly craved.

It is difficult now to imagine the pressures for social elevation that prevailed in the closing decades of the nineteenth century. Britain had achieved a global empire upon which the sun never set. The Industrial Revolution had created massive wealth from the expansion of British colonies around the world, which created apparently endless new markets for goods of every description. Suddenly there was an emergent class of industrialists and merchants: a *nouveau riche* of factory, foundry, mill and mine owners, among many other trades and services.

The middle-class Victorians from Glasgow who built the 1877 extension to this old house travelled north to the Highlands for many different reasons. They were second- and third-generation shipping merchants who had become rich by shipping people – mostly impoverished Highlanders looking for a new and better life – to the New World and bringing back to Glasgow cargoes of cheap American timber to fuel the burgeoning building trade.

The Scottish craze of the day among the leisured classes was to own at least one bank of a salmon river, a grouse moor and a slice of the hills, then to build a castle or grand sporting lodge – the most permanent and visible statement of wealth you could achieve. No country house or sporting lodge of that pretension was complete without extensive landscaped grounds and an arboretum, which, in its own way, further celebrated the colonial successes of the Victorian era with trees from colonies and dependent territories all round the world.

The giant sequoia had been accidentally 'discovered' in 1852 by a bear-hunter called Augustus T. Dowd in the Calaveros Grove in the Sierra Mountains of California (although, of course, it had been well known to Native Americans for centuries). He was astonished at the staggering size of the mature trees. One giant in particular was felled, taking a team of loggers twenty-two days to bring it down with axes and cross-cut saws. When the annual rings were counted it proved to have been 1300 years old. In a sketched and widely publicised display for the entire world to celebrate, thirty-two people were able to dance on its flat stump.

Some needly fronds and seed quickly found their way to Albert Kellogg, the botanist in residence at the newly formed Californian Academy of Sciences in San Francisco. It wouldn't be formally described until a year later; then only sneakily brought about by an English botanist determined to make his name. Commendably, Kellogg didn't want to get it wrong, so he waited until he had time to visit the mountains and see the great trees for himself. But he made the mistake of sharing his excitement with William Lobb, a visiting tree-collector sent to gather seed for an English tree nursery called Veitch & Co.

Seeing a chance to achieve immortality by attaching his name to a dramatically large species of tree new to science, Lobb behaved like a shameless cad. He slunk off to Calaveros Grove to collect his own seed and make sufficient field notes to be able to claim the credit for formally describing the new species. He dug up two small seedlings, carefully packing them in moss. Without saying a word to anyone he took ship straight back to England, arriving on 15 December 1853, and presented some of his specimens to John Lindley, professor of botanical studies at the University of London. By 24 December the official description was registered. To Lobb's well-deserved chagrin, Lindley chose to name it *Wellingtonia gigantean*, in honour of the Duke of Wellington, the national hero who had died a few months earlier.

There then ensued an international row that would run for decades. The Americans were outraged that the world's largest and oldest tree – their tree – should have been named by an English botanist who had never been to America and only seen a 'stolen' seedling. But in those days Britain's august institutions still governed the world of science, and the rules of botanical nomenclature were on Lindley's side. An impasse followed, with the Americans calling the tree *Washingtonia gigantea* and refusing to recognise anything else.

Only when the French botanist Joseph Decaisne intervened and proposed *Sequoia gigantea* did the storm begin to abate. Much later, in 1939, when it was discovered that there were significant cone and seed differences between *gigantea* and its cousin the coastal redwood, *Sequoia sempervirens*, it was again changed into a genus of its own, *Sequoiadendron*. At last everyone agreed, although to this day many people in Britain still refer to the trees as 'Wellingtonia'.

Meanwhile Veitch & Co had reproduced the tree *en masse* from the rest of Lobb's seed and turned the international botanical controversy to their commercial advantage. It became the tree everyone wanted. They made sure the seedlings were readily available; the well-to-do of every class rushed to own one or two or three . . . or six, or in the case of the Duke of Wellington's country home, Stratfield Saye, a whole avenue. They had become the botanical 'must have' of the 1870s, 1880s and 1890s, a fashion that would endure well into the twentieth century.

The legacy we enjoy at Aigas is those six fine specimen

trees among many other exotic species, now well over a hundred years old. Some have succumbed to fungal infections to which they have no resistance; others, such as the Oriental spruces and Caucasian pines, have outgrown themselves because our rainfall is greater than the much drier Continental habitats where each species evolved. The giant sequoias have also grown faster than they would have done in their much drier native California, but thankfully seem to be thriving.

★   ★   ★

It is dark. We arrive at the great tree. Arthur is on my shoulders, hanging on tight. I shine my torch up at the towering trunk of spongy bark in a tight pencil beam. The bark may be soft, but it's far from smooth. It's deeply creased with vertical ridges and thongs of ginger fibre running up for many feet, creating dark crevices, perfect for hiding in. Arthur has no real idea what we are searching for, although I have told him that the treecreeper (*Certhia familiaris*) is a small sparrow-sized bird that spends its days running up trees like a mouse, flying down and running up all over again, often in a spiral, round and round the tree. 'It's searching for insects,' I tell him. 'Tiny little insects, like spiders and flies, sometimes caterpillars.' Arthur nods knowingly, although I spot a quizzical gleam in his eye as if he is thinking, Is Grandpa having me on? I continue earnestly, 'It has a sharp little bill, curved downwards for prying and probing into cracks and crannies.'

We find several little hen's-egg-shaped indentations, all empty. Then we're in luck. There, eight feet up, now at Arthur's eye level, is a slightly ruffled bunch of brown feathers the size of a robin, apparently stuffed into a shallow cave in the bark. I have to explain to him that's it – that's a roosting treecreeper. I think he's disappointed, although he doesn't say so. It's nothing much. We can't really see that it's a bird, just the arch of its back, the feathers fluffed up against the descending cold of the autumn night.

In the morning I take him to the tree again. The bird has gone, but in the light of day we can see that the tree is dotted with little oval pits where something has carved a niche for itself out of the soft, fibrous bark. He gets the game, running round the trunk pointing up and shouting, 'Here's one . . . and another . . . Grandpa, look!'

The tree is pitted. From a few feet back I can count at least twenty of these little carvings around the huge twenty-six-foot circumference of the tree. They are all between three and twelve feet above the ground. Some, just a few, have little deposits of fresh-looking droppings at their lowest lip, a sure sign that they have recently been occupied. Off we go to explore the other five trees.

The treecreeper carves his own roosts in Sequoia bark. He does it quickly with sharp little jerks of his needle bill, occasionally scrubbing the debris out with his clawed feet. He rotates, almost as though he is building a nest, testing it for his precise size and shape. But it isn't a nest: it's a roost, a perfectly sized hollow he can tuck himself into, facing upwards so that he's warm and snug and virtually invisible. He makes several in different places on the circumference, better to avoid the shifting wind and rain. We notice that most are on the north and east, away from the prevailing wind, but crucially, others, slightly deeper, are on the west and south for when the desiccating east wind slices in from Russia and Scandinavia during the long winter months.

★   ★   ★

I am grateful to Mr J. M. D. Mackenzie, who submitted an article to the journal *Bird Study*, on 28 June 1958, entitled 'Roosting of Treecreepers'. His summary sets out his stall:

1. The roosting of treecreepers is found in Wellingtonias wherever the trees are found, although not all trees are used.
2. The roosting of treecreepers in Wellingtonia bark was first noticed in Scotland in 1905 by John Paterson.
3. The deliberate making of a roost by a special technique is thought to be unique.

The paper goes on to reveal that early in the history of the Wellingtonia presence in Britain, reports of these egg-shaped pits were emerging. To begin with, even quite celebrated naturalists were fooled. In 1907 C. H. Alston, a Highland natural history author of some repute, firmly believed that these were the work of the great spotted woodpecker:

Last year a proprietor on the shores of Loch Awe noticed that a woodpecker (*Dendrocopus major*) had most evidently been at work boring in a Wellingtonia in his grounds. The bird was never observed, but this year they have begun again on the same tree. My informant, who was lately there, saw the tree with several circular holes about 1½ in. or 2 in. diameter, not quite through the bark, some apparently freshly chipped and with white splashes of excrement round them . . . I presume that there can be little doubt but that it is the work of the Great Spotted Woodpecker.

Most evidently not. Had his informant taken the trouble to sit and watch they would quickly have seen that it was nothing to do with the woodpecker. I can't help being a little surprised that Alston, who gives the impression in his books of being very thorough, was so readily duped. But it is unkind to judge others operating in different times by the standards of our own. Two significant things were happening here in Scotland at the turn of the twentieth century.

First, the Wellingtonia trees that had been planted in the closing decades of the nineteenth were growing well and beginning to mature. I have a photograph of one of the Aigas trees taken in about 1900. A gardener, with a long white beard matching his long white apron, is leaning on a hoe, and a gardener's boy, dressed in tweed livery and wearing a tweed cap, is standing at his side. The tree is clearly visible only a few yards away. It looks to be about twenty-five feet high – growth of around twelve to fifteen inches a year. With maturity comes the depth of spongy bark, which previously had not existed as a micro-habitat in

Scotland. No British tree or any other exotic species present at that time or since possesses such a soft and fibrous protective outer layer. When the tree is young the bark is thin. Later it thickens to several inches, eventually achieving up to three feet in the real Californian giants of the Sierras. Yesterday I measured one of ours at over seven inches, a brilliant protection, insulation from mountain frosts and fire-proofing too.

Second, the great spotted woodpecker was also a relatively new species in Scotland. It was a successful bird, rapidly expanding north and exciting much interest from ornithologists and naturalists. Perhaps it isn't so surprising that Alston and his informant were not so familiar with its habits. Nowadays it is our commonest woodpecker, present in just about every wood throughout the Highlands.

Third, it was unheard of that the treecreeper might dig a pit in anything, so the notion was dismissed. As one detractor pointed out, 'The treecreeper's bill is a probe, not a pick.'

Mackenzie's paper is the more fascinating for telling us as much about birdwatchers as about the bird itself. In 1939 naturalists seemed wary of attributing new behaviour to a bird, suggesting a reluctance to accept the endlessly spinning wheel of adaptation available to every organism. It now seems obvious what the bird was up to, but clearly not so obvious to those at the time.

The Treecreeper, Mr John Simon pointed out to me, has found the dry, spongy bark of the Wellingtonia useful, presumably for nest building, and I found many – say 9-to-10 – places in the trunks where the birds had hollowed out spaces, some as neatly rounded as if a hen's egg had been half pressed into the soft bark.

Wrong again. It was nothing to do with nest-building. Treecreepers nest inside concealed crevices, not in open declivities such as the 'hen's egg' ones Mr Simon was seeing. Slowly – remarkably slowly – the world of ornithology began to work it all out. The bird had discovered a new tree and developed a new behaviour.

There is no doubt that Mr Paterson was right and that the earliest known records of roosts in Wellingtonia bark were in 1905 and 1906 in Scotland. He even uses the same simile as I did, a hen's egg. But the holes were not recognised as roosts till 1923 (N. H. Foster). The 1905–6 holes are said to be 'not quite through the bark' showing that the trees were only just big enough. In older trees to-day there is often a considerable depth of bark behind the hole. About 1907 the spread north-wards of the Great Spotted Woodpecker was being watched with interest and the work of an old resident in a new medium was taken for that of a new-comer.

Quite so. But then the penny drops properly. Mackenzie sees the whole picture:

But the Treecreeper is the only bird known to me which delib-erately makes a roosting niche used for no other purpose and using a technique different from that employed in any other activity such as nest building. The operation is taken a step further: numbers of roosts in a given area considerably exceed those of birds, so one can be used to suit the wind and weather.

★   ★   ★

It is our second night and we are out again. The moon is bright, so bright that we barely need the torch. It's just past full and lopsided on the top right as if someone has sliced a bit off. The stars are out too and it is colder, much colder, a proper autumn night. By now Arthur has seen many pictures. He knows the treecreeper intimately. He knows it lays five or six eggs in a nest of bits of bark and tiny twigs stuffed into a crevice, lined with hair and grasses. He knows it's double-brooded too, but most importantly, he understands that it carves its own niche in Sequoias. Back to the same tree; on my shoulders again. It's there again, certainly the same bird, but this time we can see it all. It's not in the same niche, but has moved north by a foot to another, deeper, pit between two thick thongs.

This time we can see it properly. I shine the torch and Arthur leans in. His face is only two feet from the bird. It turns its head to look and the needle bill is clearly visible, as is the creamy eye stripe. And it hasn't fluffed up its back feathers like last night: they're still sleek and streaky mottled like – well, like the bark it's roosting in. 'Don't move,' I whisper. I can't see Arthur's face but he is silent and still. The bird stays. I can see its glassy eye, as bright as a star in the Milky Way, reflecting my torch beam, the cream stripe running through and its long spiky tail feathers pressed against the bark.

Is five too young to see a treecreeper? Can he possibly digest what I'm showing him? Am I swamping his imagination with too much detail? Or am I imparting a tiny snippet of the joy I have known for so many years from these simple moments? We move away gently. I lower him to the ground and take his small cold hand in mine. 'Let's go and tell Mummy,' I suggest. He breaks free and runs ahead, bursting with news.

# Acknowledgements

So many to thank, so many to admire, so many loyal friends.

For general help and for just being there when I needed them: the Aigas rangers of recent years to whom I have turned over and over again for information, for details, for back-up and for support in my peculiar investigations into the natural world that governs all our lives. Phil Knot, Jenny Grant, Morag Sargent, Donald Sheilds, Brenna Boyle, Elspeth Ingleby, Ed McHugh, Jenny Campbell, Phil Taylor, Marcia Rae, Imogen German, Scott O'Hara, Duncan McNeill, Sarah Hutcheon, Hannah Thomas, Sue Hodgson, Harry Martin, Robin Noble, Amelia Williamson and Jonathan Willett.

For willing help with research and information: Sheila Kerr, Laurie Campbell, Roy Dennis, Ian Dawson, Mike Toms, Martin Davies, Melanie Evans, Miriam Darlington, Paul Ramsay, Peter Wortham, Chris Smout, Peter Tilbrook, Martha Crewe, Lesley Cranna, Polly Pullar, Ian Sargent, Vicki Saint, Ieuan Evans, Alicia Leow-Dyke, Dave Bavin, Kate Thomson, Hugh Bethune, Maciej Adamzuk, Finlay Macrae, Dave Sexton, George Swan, John Aitchison, Lennart Ardvisson, Duncan Halley, Lindsey Macrae, Nigel Bean, Jo Charlesworth, Stephen Moss, Nick Baker, Liz Holden, David Dixon and Laurie Campbell.

For inspiration: Gavin Maxwell, Sir Frank Fraser Darling, Kai Curry-Lindahl, Richard Mabey, Mark Cocker, Jim Crumley, Gary Snyder, Ted Hughes, J. A. Baker, Annie Dillard, Jane Goodall, Chris Packham, Jay Griffiths, Kathleen Jamie, Julian Clough, and a host of other naturalists, poets and nature writers, friends and mentors past and present whose works constantly swill round inside my head.

For loyalty: my generous readers, too many to name, who so kindly and thoughtfully write to me about my work; and the hundreds of field centre guests who come back year after year.

For love, tolerance and understanding: my wife Lucy, who calls herself a literary widow when I'm writing; my son Warwick, who now runs our field centre and without whose support I wouldn't have the time to write; and my daughter Hermione, who generously overlooks my perpetual distraction and absent-mindedness.

For company: the rumbustious Jack Russells, Nip and Tuck.

For joy: the blackcaps, the rooks, the red squirrels, the robins, the ravens, the pine martens and all the uplifting wildlife that frames our Aigas world and shapes our days.